Thinking about Adoption

Thinking about Adoption

A Practical and Theological Handbook
for Christians Discerning the Call to Parent
by Adoption

Karelynne Gerber Ayayo
and Michael Ayayo

CASCADE *Books* • Eugene, Oregon

THINKING ABOUT ADOPTION
A Practical and Theological Handbook for Christians Discerning the Call to Parent by Adoption

Copyright © 2017 Karelynne Gerber Ayayo and Michael Ayayo. All rights reserved. Except for brief quotations in critical publications or reviews, no part of this book may be reproduced in any manner without prior written permission from the publisher. Write: Permissions, Wipf and Stock Publishers, 199 W. 8th Ave., Suite 3, Eugene, OR 97401.

Cascade Books
An Imprint of Wipf and Stock Publishers
199 W. 8th Ave., Suite 3
Eugene, OR 97401

www.wipfandstock.com

PAPERBACK ISBN: 978-1-4982-8973-3
HARDCOVER ISBN: 978-1-4982-8975-7
EBOOK ISBN: 978-1-4982-8974-0

Cataloging-in-Publication data:

Names: Ayayo, Karelynne Gerber. | Ayayo, Michael.

Title: Thinking about adoption : a practical and theological handbook for Christians discerning the call to parent by adoption / by Karelynne Gerber Ayayo and Michael Ayayo.

Description: Eugene, OR : Cascade Books, 2017

Identifiers: ISBN 978-1-4982-8973-3 (paperback) | ISBN 978-1-4982-8975-7 (hardcover) | ISBN 978-1-4982-8974-0 (ebook)

Subjects: LCSH: Adoption—Religious aspects—Christianity.

Classification: LCC HV875.26 A9 2017 (print) | LCC HV875.26 (ebook)

Manufactured in the U.S.A.   10/19/17

For Zachary and Megan

Contents

Permissions | ix
Acknowledgments | xi
Abbreviations | xiii
Introduction | xv

1 **What is Adoption?** | 1
2 **Why Adopt? Entry Points and Motivations** | 8
3 **Private Domestic Adoption** | 18
4 **Domestic Adoption through the State** | 30
5 **Intercountry Adoption** | 39
6 **Special Needs Adoption** | 48
7 **Transracial Adoption** | 56
8 **Openness** | 65

Appendix 1 | 75
Appendix 2 | 80
Appendix 3 | 85
Appendix 4 | 91
Appendix 5 | 97
Appendix 6 | 102
Appendix 7 | 107
Appendix 8 | 112
Appendix 9 | 117
Appendix 10 | 122

Permissions

All Scripture quotations, unless otherwise indicated, are taken from the Holy Bible, New International Version®, NIV®. Copyright ©1973, 1978, 1984, 2011 by Biblica, Inc.™ Used by permission of Zondervan. All rights reserved worldwide. www.zondervan.com The "NIV" and "New International Version" are trademarks registered in the United States Patent and Trademark Office by Biblica, Inc.™

Scripture quotations marked HCSB are taken from the Holman Christian Standard Bible®, Used by Permission HCSB ©1999,2000,2002,2003,2009 Holman Bible Publishers. Holman Christian Standard Bible®, Holman CSB®, and HCSB® are federally registered trademarks of Holman Bible Publishers.

Acknowledgments

While it is our names that appear on the front of this book, an undertaking like this would have been impossible to complete on our own. We are particularly grateful to Randy Richards, Jack Kragt, and Brandon O'Brien, who from the very beginning saw potential in this project, and to colleagues at Palm Beach Atlantic University, who encouraged us along the way. To those who have shared their adoption stories with us both formally and informally, thank you. We have been so blessed. We acknowledge our families, our church family at Parkside Church Green, and our friends who graciously supported us throughout the writing process. In particular we recognize Paul and Martha Gerber, Jacob Shatzer, Nathan Lane, Kit Donald, Jen Holmes, Roy Millhouse, Jon Hinkson, and Scott Poblenz for the feedback they provided during the writing process. We further express our appreciation to Chris Spinks and the staff at Cascade for their help in bringing it all together. Thank you.

Soli Deo Gloria

Abbreviations

ASP   Adoption Service Provider
ICA   Intercountry (or International) Adoption
ICPC   Interstate Compact on the Placement of Children
MEPA   Multiethnic Placement Act
PAP   Prospective Adoptive Parent
PCSA   Public Children Services Agency
TRA   Transracial (or Interracial) Adoption
TPR   Termination of Parental Rights

Introduction

Adoption. The idea has been on your heart and mind. You have been praying about it, and you are ready to further explore what it might look like to become an adoptive parent. Congratulations! This is an exciting place to be, and the journey ahead is bound to grow you in ways that you cannot fathom, even if you never actually adopt.

After all, it is possible that you will determine that adoption is not your calling. If so, you are not alone. According to a 2013 Barna Group survey, 38 percent of practicing Christians had seriously considered adoption, but only 5 percent had actually adopted a child. That is okay. As a college professor in the field of Christian ministry, I (Karelynne) know that every student who says, "I'm called to ministry," is not called to the same ministry. There is pastoral ministry, student ministry, parachurch ministry, and more. And within each ministry is even more variety. One student minister may focus on discipleship, while another excels at evangelism.

So, too, every Christian is not expected to respond to the church's call to care for the orphan in the same way. For many it may mean serving as a child sponsor. For others it could involve a mission trip to help construct an orphanage or to run a week of Bible school. For some it will mean growing their family through adoption.

Even for those who pursue adoption, there are numerous paths forward, and not all are a good fit for everyone. It is a bit like

Introduction

decisions about where to live. Some may embrace the chance to buy a rural farmhouse complete with a pair of rocking chairs and a lazy dog on the front porch. Others foresee a house on the suburban cul-de-sac with a fire pit and pool for backyard entertaining. Still others thrive on the hustle and bustle of the downtown apartment in the big city. Where one sees a chance to garden in the peace and quiet of the country, another cringes at the thought of spending weekends mowing the yard. Where one values easy access to public transportation and local shops, another has no objection to a twenty-minute drive to get groceries.

Our family embraced the call to adopt after three years of trying but failing to conceive a child. We remember vividly the excitement we felt in the moment when we said, "Let's adopt." It was a life-changing moment, and yet nothing really happened. After all, it was not as if voicing those words was a magical formula that would cause a child to appear on our doorstep in the days ahead.

As thrilled as we were to have agreed to pursue adoption, there were doubts and unknowns. Was this really the call that God had for us? Would it work out? Practically speaking, where and how should we begin? Should we call the adoption lawyer who was recommended by a friend of a friend who had used his services ten years ago? Do we spread the word through our social networks to see if we can locate a woman who is pregnant and looking for a family to raise the baby? Should we just contact one of the agencies listed in the phone book or on the web? At that stage our awareness of the various adoption possibilities and processes was so limited that we were not even sure what questions we should be asking. We did not know what we did not know, and we wondered how to discern our next steps.

Our initial quest led us to several sources. We reached out to a handful of adoptive parents whom friends recommended to us. While their stories were interesting, their insights and advice were limited to their own experiences. Internet searches yielded an abundance of links, but identifying which ones were actually helpful for us and which information was current could turn into a full-time job. We perused a few adoption books, but they were

Introduction

filled with pages about things that simply were not relevant to us at that particular stage. It was too soon to be confronted with information about how to write a birth mother letter or what items we should pack if we were to travel to Russia to pick up a child.

It is in that context that we wished for a simple yet thoughtful resource that would introduce us to the general vocabulary and characteristics of the different kinds of adoption and that would help us to evaluate what we might find to be the advantages and disadvantages of each possibility in relation to our life circumstances and priorities. We also sought access to a wide range of stories from normal, everyday people and families who had already navigated this journey. Most importantly, we believed it was crucial to engage in solid theological reflection about adoption at every step. We wanted to meditate on biblical and theological principles alongside of practical concerns as we prayed to seek God's voice with increasing clarity.

Now more than a decade after saying "Let's adopt," both personally and professionally we have become part of the adoption community. Personally, we are among the families who have ridden the adoption roller coaster. Professionally, Michael has completed a Master of Social Work degree and now works in the field of child welfare. Karelynne has engaged in further biblical and theological study related to the topic of adoption. In short, we find ourselves equipped to provide the sort of resource that we were seeking at the beginning of our journey, and this book is the result.

Our hope is that God will use this book to minister to others who find themselves in the place where we once were. It is designed to be a first-read resource for Christians who are beginning the process of discerning whether they are called to parent by adoption. It assists the reader in answering two questions: "Might God be calling me to become an adoptive parent?" and "Which path to adoption should we pursue?"

Chapter 1 introduces adoption and provides a theological basis for understanding the significance of adoption from within a Christian worldview. Chapter 2 explores common entry points and motivations to adoption. Chapters 3–8, in turn, interact with

Introduction

various kinds of adoption: private domestic adoption (chapter 3), domestic adoption through the State (chapter 4), intercountry adoption (chapter 5), special needs adoption (chapter 6), transracial adoption (chapter 7), and open, semi-open, and closed adoption (chapter 8). Each of these chapters defines and describes the sort of adoption being discussed. It reviews the associated history and trends. It introduces theological considerations specific to the sort of adoption. It directs the reader to relevant adoptive family stories in the appendices. And it provides a corresponding reflection section to assist prospective adoptive parents (PAPs) in their own process of discernment. Finally, the appendices introduce ten Christian families who have walked the path of adoption already. The stories of their adoption decisions and processes can be read in conjunction with the various chapters, creating an adoption community that serves as a cloud of witnesses for those who are beginning the same journey.

We briefly share our story here as the foretaste of things to come. Looking back, how we eventually became parents to our son and our daughter is a bit of a blur. Ultimately, our path to becoming adoptive parents included a disrupted placement of a teenage boy, a birth mother who changed her mind about placing her newborn for adoption, and two successful interracial, private domestic adoptions of infants who have become our son and daughter.

Our process started moving forward when we connected with the local agency that placed children who were in State custody. Through them we took a training course and completed our home study. Eventually they matched us with a fourteen-year-old boy who was available to be adopted, and we prepared to become his family. We quickly began the process of meeting and then having him visit our home for increasing periods of time. The week of Thanksgiving, he finally moved in, and how thankful we were! But there would be struggles to come. After all, a childhood spent in an unhealthy family situation followed by two years in a child residential center had left their mark. He did not know what it was like to be loved. He did not know what a family was. And so it was that after being in our home for five months, the child we

Introduction

had hoped to adopt asked to return to the system to try for another family, and we had to let him go.

Even as we grieved the loss of this child, we still knew that our desire was to adopt. A friend who had done some work for a private adoption agency encouraged us in that direction. Within two months we got the call that they had a birth mother in a neighboring state who was due in two weeks. Were we interested? Interested was an understatement. We were elated! We canceled our impending summer vacation and prepared a nursery while awaiting news of the baby's birth. When the birth mother delivered, we hit the road. And so it was that we were completing some paperwork with the agency's adoption worker, mere minutes away from driving to the hospital to pick up the baby, when the phone rang. The birth mom had changed her mind about placing her baby for adoption. We returned home with empty hands and heavy hearts.

Not long after, however, our pastor attended a gathering where a representative from a local Christian children's home happened to be raising awareness about that organization. Our pastor shared our saga with the representative, and although the home did not often have infants in their care, the man said that they had an African-American infant boy whom they had not been able to place. Several weeks and numerous phone calls later, we went to meet the birth mother so that she could determine if she felt comfortable choosing us to parent her son. Talk about a surreal situation! But the meeting went well, and Zachary would become ours. He came home at the age of five-and-a-half months, and we settled in to a life of joyful sleeplessness.

That is when the saying "when it rains in pours" proved true for us. Just a week after Zachary came home, the agency that had matched us with the previous birth mother called again. There was another woman who was four months pregnant. Because the baby's gender and race were unknown, they had no other families expressing interest. Would we be open to adopting this child? We thought we must be crazy to take two babies in less than a year! They would be only eleven months apart in age, an arrangement that is barely possible in biological families. Yet we did want more than one child.

Introduction

And after all we had been through, why say no when God seemed to be opening the door? There might be advantages to having the two children so close in age. So we agreed. Nearly six years after beginning our attempts to have a family, Megan was born and came home with us when she was two days old.

The story did not end when the adoption decrees were finalized. As we have moved from process to parenting, there have been some surprises. Most notably, at age two, our son was diagnosed as being on the autism spectrum. Although we did not know it at the beginning, we had become a special needs family. Also unexpected have been chances to interact with our daughter's siblings, and we do not yet know how those relationships may develop in the years ahead.

Without a doubt, our call to parent by adoption has required sacrifice. It is equally true that it has brought blessing. Reality has replaced romanticism along the bumpy road of our adoption journey, but God continues to strengthen and sustain us along the way. We pray that you also will find yourself drawing closer to God as you explore adoption options and discern the call he may have for you.

1

What is Adoption?

As we think deeper about adoption, we start by defining it, considering significant historical and biblical backgrounds, and engaging in initial theological reflections. Generally, the word "adoption" speaks about a process by which a person secures a permanent parent-child relationship by means of legal pronouncement rather than by birth. Adoption involves *biological parents*, who may be called first, natural, or birth parents. The *adoptee*, typically a child, is born to the biological parents but at some point is placed for adoption and raised by *adoptive parents*. Together these three parties comprise an *adoption triad* or an *adoption triangle*.

A variety of adoptive practices exist including kinship or fictive kinship adoption, non-relative adoption, and international adoption. Some children are adopted by family members. These kinship adoptions may involve grandparents adopting a grandchild, an aunt and uncle parenting a niece or nephew due to the death, inability, or absence of the biological parent, or even a stepparent putting in place a legal relationship with the child of a spouse. We find a biblical parallel to kinship adoption in Esther, who was raised by her cousin after the death of her parents (Esth 2:7). A fictive kinship adoption involves the placement of a child

Thinking about Adoption

with a known family friend who may already be treated as family. If Abraham had remained childless, his selection of Eliezer to be his heir would reflect something of a fictive kinship adoption (Gen 15:3). Today many children are adopted by people who are unfamiliar to them. Legal documentation of this type of adoption in the United States began in the 1920s. Racially, culturally, and geographically, adoptees may come from a place of close proximity to or of great distance from the adoptive parents, including other countries. Moses provides a biblical example of an adoption in which the adoptive parent and child possessed geographical closeness, but a racial and cultural divide (Exod 2:10).

Adoption was practiced at least informally in the ancient world, including in biblical times, although it often focused primarily on issues of inheritance rather than on the needs of a child. For example, the Roman emperor Julius Caesar adopted his great-nephew Octavian, but he only did so upon his death in order to name an heir to his rule and fortune since he lacked direct male descendants.

The seeds of modern adoption practices were planted in the United States when Massachusetts passed the first adoption law in 1851. This law required a judge to confirm that a legal guardian or kin consented in writing to the placement of a child, that the adoptive family was capable of raising the child, and that the adoption was fit and proper. It also documented that the child gained full membership in the adoptive family with rights of inheritance and succession.

In the decades that followed, the United States witnessed significant numbers of orphans due to war, immigration, and poverty. Both public and private systems emerged to address the needs of orphans. The placement of children in homes with foster families began as an alternative to institutional orphanages, and so-called orphan trains moved children from the East to the Midwest in hopes of finding adoptive families. By the mid-twentieth century, governmental regulation of adoptions and the involvement

What is Adoption?

of adoption agencies in the placement of children had increased greatly.

The University of Oregon's Adoption History Project reports that the number of formal adoptions in the United States peaked in 1970 at approximately one hundred seventy-five thousand per year, but it has declined to around one hundred twenty-five thousand annually thereafter.[1] Overall, families that include an adopted child remain quite rare. The 2010 Census reports that just 2.4 percent of householders in the United States had adopted children under the age of eighteen living in the home at that time.[2] A 2013 Barna Groups survey reveals that those who identify as practicing Christians adopt at twice the rate of the average adult (5 percent), while Catholics are three times and evangelicals are five times as likely to adopt as the general population.[3]

BIBLICAL OBSERVATIONS

The Bible engages adoption in two distinct ways. First, it records the adoption of specific people like Moses and Esther as seen above. It may be that the relationships between Jacob and his grandsons Ephraim and Manasseh (Gen 48:5–6), between Naomi and Obed (Ruth 4:16–17), and between Tahpenes and Genubath (1 Kgs 11:20) can be viewed through the lens of adoption.

Second, adoption stands among the many rich biblical metaphors that reveal truths about God's relationship with his redeemed people. All those who have the indwelling Spirit of God have received a spirit of adoption (*huiothesia*, which literally means "placement as sons," Rom 8:15) and are rightly designated as children of God (John 1:12, 1 John 3:1), not by natural birth but because of God's love and by God's initiative (John 1:13, Eph 1:4–5).

---

1. http://pages.uoregon.edu/adoption/topics/adoptionstatistics.htm.
2. https://www.census.gov/prod/2014pubs/p20-572.pdf.
3. https://www.barna.com/research/5-things-you-need-to-know-about-adoption/.

Thinking about Adoption

God's decision to adopt key people or groups is evident throughout the biblical story. God's call to Abram hints of adoption as Abram leaves his father's household and is promised an inheritance from the Lord (Gen 12:1; 24:7). Through the exodus from Egyptian slavery, God adopts corporate Israel as his son (Exod 4:22; Jer 31:9; Hos 11:1; Rom 9:4), and he is named as Israel's father (Isa 64:8). An adoption formula appears in Psalm 2:7 with reference to the Davidic king (see also 2 Sam 7:14–15), and 1 Chronicles 28:6 narrates its specific application to King Solomon. The New Testament shows that God's adoptive family includes Christians regardless of their ethnic background. Gentile believers are part of the household of God as full heirs alongside of believing Israel (John 11:52; Eph 2:19; 3:6; Rom 9:25–26).

Three additional details stand out in Scripture's picture of adoption. First, adoption is often presented as a transformation from slavery to sonship, either literal slavery in Egypt (Exod 6:6b–7) or a life of spiritual slavery (Gal 4:3–7; Rom 8:15). Second, the biblical presentation confirms that the adopted child is a full, legal member of the family, who already has the associated rights and privileges of family membership and who anticipates an inheritance of all that God has promised (Rom 8:17). Third, it recognizes some challenges of living as an adoptive family (Jer 3:19). Those who are adopted into God's family are called to embrace their new relationships and status (1 John 3:2; Rom 8:15). They should begin to develop a family resemblance as they conform to the image of Christ (Rom 8:29) and live a life led by the Spirit, which is the distinguishing mark of one's membership in God's family (Rom 8:14). Similarly, God models the kind of love, compassion, and patience that may be required of an adoptive parent toward children who struggle with their identity and call (Hos 11:1–7).

THEOLOGICAL REFLECTIONS

As with all metaphors, human (horizontal) adoption cannot fully mimic its spiritual (vertical) counterpart. For instance, in spiritual adoption, God powerfully transforms his children into new

What is Adoption?

creations (2 Cor 5:17). Human adoption does no such thing. In similar fashion, Christ genuinely saves his bride, the church, while human husbands do not save their wives (Eph 5:23). Nonetheless, human practices like adoption and marriage exist as a means for Christians to bear witness, however imperfectly, to their divine counterparts, and they are most successful when they are undertaken in light of theological reflection on the corresponding biblical metaphor.

Theological reflection on the biblical image of the Christian's spiritual adoption provides several insights for the literal practice of adoption. First, it offers a model both for adoption as the reunification or reconciliation of an alienated child with the original parent and also for adoption as the placement of a child into a new family.

God is the Creator of all beings. Thus, in some sense, God occupies the role of first parent of humanity as a whole (Deut 32:6; Isa 43:5-6). The fall of mankind into sin alienated and orphaned creature from Creator, but God reconciles with those whom he adopts and brings them back into a rightful relationship with their heavenly Father. In this regard, adoption as reunification makes sense of the relationship between God and mankind collectively.

On an individual level, however, it is equally true that all people born after the fall never actually experience God as their first parent because they are born into original sin. Rather, the Bible suggests that the devil functions as the spiritual father of those who are unregenerate (John 8:44; Acts 13:10; 1 John 3:8, 10). Those who are saved and adopted by God leave their birth parent and find a family among brothers and sisters in the Kingdom of God. Biblical texts that speak of salvation with the language of rebirth (John 3:3-7; 1 Pet 1:23) and new identity (2 Cor 5:17) further support the idea of adoption as placement.

Such reflection provides a helpful reminder that as Christians attempt to look after orphans (Jas 1:27), we can minister best to some children by providing them with adoptive families. At the same time we can also embrace efforts that aim to reunify alienated children with their birth parents, with their extended families, or with their communities of origin if it is possible and in the best interests of the child.

Second, the very concept of adoption does not exist apart from the presence of sin in the world (Gen 3). People in a sinless world would naturally live in God's family, as Adam and Eve did during their earliest days in the Garden of Eden. They would have no need for spiritual adoption. Similarly, in such a world void of death, war, poverty, disease, rape, abuse, incarceration, sexual immorality, gender selection, and neglect, all children would be born to parents who are willing and able to raise them well. Likewise, people who desire to parent would be able to do so without the pain of infertility, miscarriage, or the death of a child.

By application, this truth reminds potential adoptive parents (PAPs) that all adoption has its starting point in the realities of sin, grief, or loss. All the members of the adoption triad may feel a mix of joy and sorrow. A mindful adoption acknowledges this ambiguity and creates space for biological parents, adoptees, and adoptive parents to grieve the losses they experience.

Finally, creation and adoption are both beautiful, but different, ways to glorify God. Theologically speaking, procreation is planted in God's economy of creation. Those who come into a parenting relationship with their children biologically are invited to participate most directly in those elements of God's story that are creative. They literally fulfill the creation mandate (Gen 1:22), and they create children in their own image (Gen 1:27–28).

Adoption belongs within God's economy of redemption whereby God transforms the slave into a son (John 8:35; Gal 4:7), replaces curse with blessing (Zech 8:13; Eph 1:3), restores the downtrodden and vulnerable (Zech 10:6), and brings beauty from ashes (Isa 61:3). Although adoption is secondary to creation, it is not second best. Through adoption, believers are invited to live out the story of redemption in a profound and intimate way within their own family.

What is Adoption?

REFLECT AND RESPOND

- What surprises you most about the history of adoption? About the statistics of adoption?

- How do the concepts of spiritual adoption and redemption affect and inform your understanding of literal adoption?

- As a Christian, reflect on your experience of salvation in relation to the metaphor of adoption. What does it mean to you to identify as a child of God by adoption?

2

Why Adopt?

Entry Points and Motivations

Why adopt? In one sense, our family can answer that we adopted because we wanted children, but we were unable to conceive on our own. But that is not the whole picture. Ultimately, we determined that God was calling us to become adoptive parents. We were sensitive to our identity as adopted children of God, and we had both the longing and the ability to parent by adoption. Infertility was merely one of the means through which our ears became better able to hear God's call for us.

Similarly, when prospective adoptive parents (PAPs) weigh the reasons that they might adopt, we recommend that they approach their decision in terms of discernment and calling. Adoption is best pursued by people who are called to do so, yet discerning a calling is not always easy. While some may receive, and others may desire, a direct, audible voice from the Lord, more often God sovereignly extends the particular call to adoption and moves people to respond as the needs of the world, the desires and burdens of their hearts, and God's Word intersect.

Why Adopt?

These three elements often whisper together in the hearts and minds of PAPs. Available data confirm that some orphans around the world have a genuine need for adoptive families. Certain life contexts commonly motivate people to consider adoption as a possibility for their families. Additionaly, the biblical principle of overflow allows the Christian experience of spiritual adoption to serve as a primary foundation for Christians to become adoptive parents.

THE NEED

An astonishing number of children around the world are classified as orphans because they have lost one (single orphan) or both (double orphan) of their parents. Although precise numbers are impossible to come by, a 2013 report by UNICEF, UNAIDS, and WHO estimates that more than one hundred fifty million children around the world are either single or double orphans.[1] The Christian Alliance for Orphans white paper on understanding orphan statistics cautions that these numbers fail to reflect the additional millions of social orphans who may have two living parents but who reside in institutions or on the streets without meaningful contact with family.[2] Within the United States itself, the Department of Health and Human Services Administration for Children and Families reports that there are at least one hundred thousand children in foster care each year who are waiting to be adopted.[3] The circumstances that each of these young people face vary greatly, but many of them remain among the most vulnerable children in the world.

    1. UNICEF, UNAIDS, and WHO. Children and AIDS: Sixth Stocktaking Report. 2013. http://www.unaids.org/sites/default/files/media_asset/20131129_stocktaking_report_children_aids_en_0.pdf.

    2. Christian Alliance for Orphans White Paper: On Understanding Orphan Statistics. https://cafo.org/wp-content/uploads/2015/10/Orphan-Statistics-Web-9-2015.pdf.

    3. http://www.acf.hhs.gov/sites/default/files/cb/children_waiting2012.pdf.

Thinking about Adoption

Adoption should not be promoted as the only or even the best way to minister to these children. Some will never legally be freed to be adopted. Others can benefit the most from solutions that enable them to reunite or remain with a living parent or member of their extended family. Nonetheless, adoption should not be overlooked as part of the Christian response for the many children in the United States and around the world who are without permanent caregivers.

OUR MOTIVATIONS

The specific combination of factors that may lead a person to consider becoming an adoptive parent can be as diverse as the people themselves. At times, an awareness of the needs of orphans is the driving force, and PAPs feel the burden to respond with compassion and empathy. In other situations, the longing of the adoptive parents is the primary motivation. They want to have a child but may face roadblocks to a natural birth. Alternatively, some people's desires to adopt grow as a result of positive interactions with others who have been part of the adoption process already. Each context comes with its own cautions because, as fallen creatures, our human motivations to adopt can be tainted by sin. Thus, PAPs need deep self-reflection and honesty in their discernment process.

Motivation 1: "Every child deserves a loving family." "There are needy children in the world."

Sad eyes. Skin and bones. A contorted body. Faces peering through the bars of a gate. A room crowded with cribs. From AIDS orphans and girls abandoned simply because they are girls, to victims of poverty and children who bear the scars of war or the misfortune of physical deformities, gripping photos depict the plight of many orphans around the world. Closer to home, television and radio advertisements ring in our ears. Children in our own

Why Adopt?

communities, who are victims of abuse or neglect, are waiting for forever families.

Such images and stories are compelling. They speak to the heart and can lead sensitive souls to declare their desire to adopt every available child! These are the PAPs who are drawn to adoption because they have become aware of a need and feel that they must do something to help. Compassion and pity drive them forward as they seek to be the hands and feet of Jesus for the least of these.

The challenge with this motivation is to have realistic expectations. Adoption is about a child and not about a cause. Such a life-long commitment calls for sober-mindedness, and the head must temper the heart. Along with considering their ability to offer love, meet basic needs, and provide stability, PAPs should recognize that children who come from challenging beginnings—for instance, institutionalization and abuse—often require additional resources and different parenting strategies. It is tempting for adoptive parents to assume a savior mentality or think that adoptees will respond with gratitude. PAPs may assert that love will overcome any hurts the children have experienced, but the reality is often quite different, and there is the risk of great harm when an adoptee does not live up to the unrealistic expectations of the adoptive parents. Emotion alone is rarely enough to overcome the difficulties that can arise. Therefore, in the desire to meet the needs of orphans, prospective parents do well to consider fully the many ways that they might serve vulnerable children before determining whether adoption is the call God has for them.

Motivation #2: "We cannot get pregnant." "My doctor has warned us that a pregnancy could endanger my health." "We face a high genetic risk." "We have lost a baby."

Although the specific details associated with each of the scenarios differ, in every case couples want to have children but face circumstances that make it unlikely, impossible, or traumatic for them to bear them biologically. The good news is that adoption can provide

Thinking about Adoption

a path to parenting. Friends who know their struggles may even tell them, "You can always adopt." Nonetheless, treating adoption as the automatic next step or default response to these challenges is unwise. Parenting by adoption is best approached as an intentional choice rather than as a last resort or a back-up plan.

Couples who begin to consider adoption because of the reasons outlined above may have an increased risk of improperly viewing the adopted child as a means to fulfill their own emotional needs. Therefore they are encouraged first to take time to acknowledge and grieve their losses. It may seem obvious that those who have miscarried or lost a child after birth will need to mourn for the children who have died. Adoption cannot replace these precious ones. But there is grief even for those who have not lost a particular child. A decision to adopt asks them to give up a dream or exchange one life script for another. Adoption may provide a child, but the adoptive mother will not get to feel a baby move inside her belly. She will not join the sisterhood of women who have endured the anguish and joy of childbirth. The adoptive father will not live up to cultural stereotypes regarding virility and manhood. He may mourn the loss of legacy that is associated with biological fatherhood and the creation of a "mini-me" who carries on the family genes.

Furthermore, adopting is not merely a decision to parent, but to parent in a particular kind of way, and those who proceed will need to count the cost. This is true in terms of finances since adoption can be expensive, and couples may have already spent thousands of dollars on medical diagnoses and treatments. It is also true with regard to the many additional factors that make parenting by adoption different from having a natural child. Adoptive parents can expect to miss portions of their child's life since they are absent from the period prior to the child's placement, whether it be a few days, months, or years. They cannot control the child's prenatal environment but will have to address any lingering effects of drug exposure or malnutrition. They may receive little to no information about the child's family of origin, or conversely, they may find themselves embracing the idea of a blended family to

Why Adopt?

make space for long-term interactions with members of the family of origin or other significant caregivers who were in the adoptee's life prior to placement.

Such factors should caution couples to think through whether their desire to have children is compatible with parenting by adoption, or whether they might prefer to seek out involvement with children by being the awesome aunt, mentoring at-risk youth, volunteering in the children's ministry at church, or in some other way.

Motivation #3: "I have never gotten married."

Adoption may appeal to single adults who find themselves wanting to parent, but such individuals should not pursue adoption in an attempt to fulfill unmet relational needs. They may also need to take extra care as they assess whether they have the necessary time, money, and support systems in place to enable them to parent well without a partner.

Despite these practical concerns, there may be instances when a single parent emerges as a good match for a particular adoptee. The teenaged girl who has been sexually abused by male relatives, for instance, may transition to a home with a single mother far more easily than she would to a two-parent family. In all instances, the actual children being placed should be matched carefully to ensure that a single-parent home provides a setting in which they can feel loved and secure, and be able to thrive.

Motivation #4: "We have five boys already, and we would really like to have a girl." "We want to be a multicultural family."

Whereas biological parents have no ethical options to engage in gender selection, and children do always emerge from the birth canal as newborns, PAPs can specify the age, gender, and race of their child. They may have good reasons to prefer a girl or not to take a child under age five, but when the ability to get a particular sort of child stands as the primary motive for adoption, there may be cause for concern. For instance, it is selfish and prejudiced to adopt an older child in order to avoid sleepless nights or the process of potty training, or to specify an Asian child in hopes that she will be smart. Furthermore, PAPs will want to avoid a consumer mindset. Most stores allow consumers to exchange or return purchases when they do not fit right or fail to perform as expected. However, carrying this mentality into an adoption is inappropriate, increases the chances of a disrupted placement, and can only bring additional pain and grief to hurting children who feel that they do not measure up.

Motivation #5: "My sister was adopted." "Our friends just adopted a baby."

Other couples may consider adoption because they have family members or close friends who are either adoptees or adoptive parents. When adoption feels familiar, people are more likely to think of it as a means of growing their own families. PAPs may even be adoptees themselves and believe that the adoption was a positive experience for everyone involved. The caution here is that not all adoptions will be the same. PAPs should not assume that their experience will proceed the way that others' have. They also may need to consider whether they are thinking about adopting out of a sense of obligation because it is what their family expects, or because of its trendiness, particularly in evangelical Christian circles.

GOSPEL MOTIVATIONS FROM GOD'S WORD

The kindness and blessings that God bestows on his children fill us to such an extent that when we truly recognize such things, we find that we cannot contain them, but that they spill over into the lives of those around us. Because we are loved by God, we can love others (1 John 4:19). Because we are humbly served by Christ, we

Why Adopt?

can humbly serve those around us (John 13:12–17). This is the biblical principle of overflow.

The apostle Paul similarly expresses this idea. Writing to believers in Corinth, he erupts in doxology: "Praise be to the God and Father of our Lord Jesus Christ, the Father of compassion and the God of all comfort, who comforts us in all our troubles" (2 Cor 1:3–4a). Yet he does not stop there. He recognizes that God's work in our lives has implications for how we as believers can and should respond to others. "So that we can comfort those in any trouble with the comfort we ourselves receive from God . . . our comfort abounds through Christ" (2 Cor 1:4b–5), or in the words of the Holman Christian Standard Bible translation, "through Christ our comfort also overflows." Christians can give out of the abundance of what God has given to us.

At one time, we all lived as spiritual orphans in desperate need of love, acceptance, protection, guidance, and discipline. God met us in our distress and comforted us by becoming our Father and naming us as his children. He adopted us. Therefore, believers have the ability to extend adoption to others as the overflow of our own experience. We need not adopt out of obligation, or duty, or as an attempt to obey a particular biblical teaching, but we can adopt out of a profound sense that this is what God has enabled us to do because he has already done it for us.

Although being adopted in Christ provides a Christian foundation for adopting children, not all Christians are called to become adoptive parents. Adoption is but one of the many rich metaphors that Scripture uses to describe the Christian's experience of salvation. The concept can provide theological insight for all believers. Yet some find that the Spirit of God continually draws their hearts and minds to it until the reality of their spiritual adoption emerges as a dominant and defining truth in their lives.

So why adopt? It is certainly possible to approach adoption as a simple good work or a means to personal fulfillment. However, as Christians who see the needs of the world, honestly evaluate our own desires and burdens, and reflect on how God's abundant grace in our own lives can overflow, we may find a far better answer. We adopt because we have discerned a call from God.

REFLECT AND RESPOND

- How do you understand calling? How have you heard God's calling in your life before? How might you hear it now?

- What has motivated you to consider adoption? Describe the circumstances that have led you to this point.

- Are you interested in any organizations or programs that minister to orphans and vulnerable children? How might you get involved in these (if you are not already)?

Why Adopt?

- Do you have any losses that you need to grieve before you would be able to move forward with adoption in a healthy way? How might you do that?

- Can you identify any selfish or impure motives in your desire to adopt?

- Do you know other people who have adopted or been adopted? Describe what you know about their experiences.

3

Private Domestic Adoption

"Pick me." I (Karelynne) would whisper these words under my breath when it came time to choose teams in middle school gym class. But as the smallest girl in the class, frequently I would watch the ranks of the chosen grow while I waited to hear my name. Why couldn't I be chosen? Ironically, I had quite different feelings in high school English class when the teacher called on students to share their work aloud. I would shrink down in my desk and avoid eye contact in hopes of escaping his notice. I dreaded being singled out from my classmates, and I feared what the teacher might say if I did not meet his expectations. Why did I have to be chosen?

I am equally conflicted when I am the one making choices. When we built our house, I spent several hours deliberating over more than twenty paint chips, all variations of red, for the color of our front door alone. It was overwhelming. But as a picky eater, I can feel frustrated when I attend events with limited food choices. Having to decide whether to eat what is offered or to go hungry does not feel like much of a choice. I want more options!

When it comes to human experiences of choosing and being chosen, clearly there are conflicting emotions in play. Since the term adoption itself derives from a Latin word meaning to choose,

Private Domestic Adoption

we would be naïve to think that the members of the adoption triad are devoid of similar ambivalence in relationship to adoption. Choice should imply autonomy and freedom, but adoption frequently leaves people feeling rejected, insecure, overwhelmed, and powerless. Private domestic adoption, which is the focus of this chapter, brings out these complicated dynamics perhaps more than any other path to adoption.

The phrase *domestic adoption* refers to adoptions that place American-born children with adoptive parents who also live in the United States. Domestic adoptions occur in both the public and private sectors. Government-sponsored social service entities facilitate *public domestic adoptions* involving children from within the child welfare system (see chapter 4), while non-governmental providers work with *private domestic adoptions*. Because private domestic adoption usually involves the placement of infants rather than older children, it may be called *infant adoption*.

WHERE DO (ADOPTEE) BABIES COME FROM?

From the single teenager to the young professional or the married mother of five, women in a wide variety of life circumstances experience unplanned pregnancies. As they consider the road ahead, some determine that they are unprepared to raise the child in the way that they would want, and they turn to adoption. Expectant mothers can use their own connections to identify a family who would like to adopt the infant. They can partner with an adoption service provider (ASP) to make an adoption plan in which they may outline generally the sort of family that they want the child to have or even select specific adoptive parents from among a provider's waiting families. Alternatively, birth parents can follow Safe Haven laws in their state that may allow them to surrender their newborn anonymously to designated Safe Haven providers like hospitals or fire stations. In all of these cases, infants are legally relinquished by their biological parents and become available for private domestic adoption.

Thinking about Adoption

ADOPTION SERVICE PROVIDERS

Those who seek to adopt such infants cannot do it alone. You will need to work with an adoption service provider to complete either an agency adoption, an independent adoption, or some hybrid of the two. In *agency adoptions*, for-profit or nonprofit adoption agencies licensed by your state provide a full range of services to birth parents and prospective adoptive parents (PAPs). In *independent adoptions*, adoption attorneys advise and assist PAPs.

In many ways, the differences between independent adoptions and agency adoptions are like the differences between planning your own vacation and purchasing a package from a travel agent. Managing all of the details yourself requires significant time and attention, but you can often customize your trip, face fewer restrictions, and maybe even get a better deal. Using a travel agency is convenient if you do not have the time, ability, or interest to select and coordinate airfare, transfers, lodging, and activities all through separate vendors. Someone else oversees all of the details for you, and you have some protection or recourse if something goes wrong.

Plan to research and interview multiple ASPs. As you explore independent providers, we recommend that you consider how many adoptions they have completed, whether they belong to the American Academy of Adoption Attorneys, and how familiar they are with the adoption laws not only of your state of residence but also of any state from which you might want to adopt. Clarify which specific adoption services they perform as well as the estimated costs, although be aware that difficult legal situations or unexpected developments can quickly increase fees. Finally, ask what parts of the adoption process are your responsibility, and seek the attorney's guidance about any state-specific laws and restrictions that govern the steps you will need to take. Remember that these can be complicated and time-consuming, and you can expect to incur additional expenses.

When considering private adoption agencies, larger agencies offer and may even require orientation sessions for the purpose of

Private Domestic Adoption

answering common questions from PAPs. You can gather information by attending an orientation, reviewing an agency's published materials, or interacting with a staff member. Take the time to investigate what kinds of adoption programs are offered, any eligibility requirements that exist to apply (age, marital status, number of children, etc.), how much experience the agency and its current staff have, and whether the agency is national or licensed for child placement only in particular states. Ask how they find and screen their birth parents, what services they provide to them, and how they match birth parents with adoptive families.

> "We interviewed quite a few agencies in our state ... We wanted to have a clear conscience and rejoice in the adoption process while knowing that the birth parents were well treated."
> —An adoptive mother (Appendix 3)

Agencies can differ markedly when it comes to both the time and cost involved with an adoption. In your research it is helpful to compare the average number of placements the agency makes annually in each program, how many families are currently on their active waiting list, and the average amount of time PAPs wait before being matched with a birth mother and/or before having a child placed with them. You will want to look at the average cost for adopting through each program, but also the accounting breakdown, how fees are determined, when fees are due, and whether monies are refunded, credited, or lost if an adoption fails. It is not unusual for agencies to charge for costs associated with advertising, birth parent services, birth mother living expenses (if legal in your state), adoptive parent screening and training, social worker services, and legal matters. An agency adoption easily can cost upwards of $25,000, and PAPs may have extra expenses for travel, background screening, and legal services to finalize the adoption.

If possible, interview several other families who have adopted through each ASP you consider, and check with the Better Business Bureau, the State Attorney's General Office, and the State Licensing Specialist to see if any complaints have been filed against the

Thinking about Adoption

ASP. Beyond such facts, evaluate how easy it is to get in touch with the ASP and whether you feel like they take the time to answer your questions. All of these factors should help you to identify an adoption service provider with whom you feel comfortable and to avoid unnecessary surprises if you move forward.

WHAT TO EXPECT WITH A PRIVATE ADOPTION

All adoptions are unique, but many private domestic adoptions share a basic vocabulary and general process including the home study, adoptive family profile, matching, consents, placement, probationary period, and finalization. If you discern that God is calling you to domestic private adoption, you will become intimately familiar with each of these elements.

An adoption agency cannot place a child in your home unless you have a current, approved *home study*. Federal and state laws, along with policies put in place by your ASP, will outline the particulars for your home study process. The average home study takes three to six months to complete and remains valid for six to twenty-four months, depending on state law. Some PAPs may need to update their home study during the adoption process.

For your home study, an approved assessor will interview you about your family composition, background, education, employment, parenting style, interests, and motivations for adoption. A home visit will determine whether you have a suitable home environment that meets established safety standards (working smoke detectors, fencing around swimming pools, etc.) and includes a designated space that will become the baby's room.

You will submit official documentation, including birth certificates, marriage licenses, and divorce certificates, if applicable. Because the safety of children is paramount, PAPs are fingerprinted and undergo criminal background checks, and certain felonies (including convictions for causing harm to a child) will disqualify you from adopting. Although you are not required to be wealthy, your W2s, bank statements, or income tax forms should demonstrate that you are financially responsible enough to provide for the basic needs of a child. A medical evaluation will confirm that you are in general good health and not afflicted with any untreated conditions that would interfere with your ability to parent a child.

During the home study period you can expect to complete a designated number of hours of training that introduce more details about the legalities and process of adoption, the impact of adoption on adoptees, birth parent relationships, cultural issues, resources for parenting the adopted child, and similar topics. You will make decisions about your adoption preferences (many agencies will provide an actual preference form for you to use), if any, with regard to the race, culture, age, and gender of the child, the number of children you are willing to accept at one time (for instance, twins or sibling groups), and the amount of ongoing interaction with the birth family. You will determine your openness with regard to the medical background of the birth parents, including matters such as the level of prenatal care the birth mother received, or whether the baby was exposed to particular drugs or alcohol during the pregnancy. And you will specify if you are willing to accept a child with known physical disabilities, mental disorders, developmental delays, or other special needs.

> "There were nearly fifty different things that we had to decide! It felt so unnatural and took a while for us to process."
> —An adoptive mother (Appendix 4)

It can feel daunting, intrusive, and even unfair to be placed under the home study microscope. After all, biological parents face none of these requirements. However it is worth keeping in mind that ASPs generally want to help PAPs successfully navigate the home study process and be approved to adopt. You do not need to be perfect, but you should expect to be truthful and self-reflective.

Alongside of the home study, many PAPs complete a scrapbook of sorts, called an *adoptive parent profile* for the purpose of introducing themselves to a birth family. Typical profiles include a letter to the birth mother plus photos and narratives that tell not only facts about your family and home but also display your personality, interests, traditions, and hopes for adopting. Your profile does not need to be fancy, but it should be thoughtful and honest. You may be surprised at what it is that will draw a birth parent to you!

A *match* occurs when PAPs and expectant mothers agree to work exclusively with one another toward an adoption plan. Although a match is a serious step toward adoption, it is not legally binding. Expectant parents may reverse their decision for any reason, and PAPs can, and sometimes do, walk away from a match.

> "Later we learned that we stood out to Kayleigh's birth mother because our pet rabbit had the same name as her pet dog. Here I was expecting something like, 'Their love of Jesus just came through' or something equally profound!"
> —An adoptive mother (Appendix 3)

Agencies facilitate the matching process by including your adoptive parent profile among those that are on their active waiting list. The wait time for a match is unpredictable and can vary considerably due to the size of your agency, their policies about how many family profiles they present to each birth family and in what order they present them, and how limited or flexible your own adoption preferences are.

In independent adoptions, PAPs have greater involvement in locating a birth mother, but they must be careful to follow relevant state laws. Some states permit attorneys to assist in matching PAPs with birth mothers, and most states permit PAPs to draw on help from family, friends, doctors, or pastors, as long as they are not paid for their assistance. Few states allow the use of paid, unlicensed adoption facilitators.

Birth parents must sign *consents*, sometimes called surrenders or relinquishments, to terminate their parental rights in order to free their child legally for adoption. Although some states permit birth parents, particularly fathers, to sign surrenders prior to the baby's birth, many designate a period of time after birth, often seventy-two hours, before a mother is permitted to make voluntary

Private Domestic Adoption

consent. Additional consent may be required from a birth mother's husband, even if he is not the baby's father, or from the parents of a birth mother, if she is a minor. States specify whether a written, notarized statement is sufficient, whether a birth parent must appear before a judge to consent to the adoption, and whether birth parents must be provided with counseling or with a lawyer prior to consent.

After signing consents, some states grant birth parents a period of time, ranging from forty-eight hours to several months, during which they can revoke their surrenders and resume custody of their child without having to demonstrate their consents were signed under fraud or duress.

A child who is legally free to be adopted can be placed into the home of approved PAPs. Many families refer to the *placement day* as "Gotcha Day," and they may celebrate the anniversary in special ways throughout the adoptee's life.

PAPs who adopt a child born outside of their home state must clear the Interstate Compact on the Placement of Children (ICPC) in order to bring the baby home. Under the ICPC, the home study that was completed and approved in your state of residence must be sent to and accepted by the child's home state before the child is cleared to leave his/her state, and this approval period often takes one to two weeks.

Having a child placed in your home is not the same thing as a finalized adoption. After placement, states require a *probationary period* of various lengths (six months is a typical minimum) during which your adoption worker will make regular visits to your home to observe and interview the family about your adjustment to the new child. The worker can direct you to additional services that may assist you in this time of transition.

You will need to go before a judge to complete, or finalize, your adoption. Once you have satisfied all of the legal requirements for

> "After going through such a lengthy adoption process, we were amused that we spent less than 60 seconds in the courtroom for the finalization!"
> —An adoptive mom (Appendix 4)

adoption in your state, you petition the court for permission to adopt the child. The *finalization* of a domestic adoption occurs when the court issues an adoption decree stating that the adoptive parents are granted permanent, legal custody of the adoptee.

IS PRIVATE DOMESTIC ADOPTION A GOOD FIT FOR ME?

Private domestic adoption is a particularly good fit for PAPs who have located a birth mother who is willing to place her child with them in an identified adoption. Because private domestic adoption is virtually the only means of adopting a newborn, it attracts PAPs who seek to raise a child from infancy. If you have very limited preferences, and are looking to adopt a Caucasian female with no known exposure to drugs or alcohol, for instance, you would follow this path. Because private domestic adoption does carry a high financial cost, and the wait for a child is often long and unpredictable, it is less ideal for PAPs who have limited finances or who prioritize a quick placement. Finally, the overwhelming majority of private domestic adoptions being done now include some ongoing interaction between the adoptive family and the family of origin. PAPs who object to this may do better with other options.

THEOLOGICAL CONSIDERATIONS

Within God's economy of redemption, spiritual adoption is a joint act of God and the adoptee, which is marked by at least three characteristics worth exploring here. First, those who enter into spiritual adoption do so as free and willing participants. God lovingly and willfully adopts out of his absolute sovereign freedom and for his own pleasure (Eph 1:3–5, Phil 2:13). Also, as God's grace works in concert with human will, believers exercise genuine freedom as we come near to Christ in repentance and faith (Matt 11:28, Mark 1:15). Although theologians attempt to explain the intricacies of this relationship, Scripture seems content to present both realities

Private Domestic Adoption

without fully harmonizing them or revealing the mystery. Second, spiritual adoption is unconditional, unmerited, and by grace. God's choices are not contingent upon the ancestry, actions, or accomplishments of his children (Eph 2:8–9). Finally, spiritual adoption is irreversible and eternally secure (Eph 1:13, John 10:27–30).

The Christian hope is that human adoption bears witness to these truths of spiritual adoption, but all too often human adoption falls short of these principles, resulting in pain and grief for members of the adoption triad. For instance, in private domestic adoptions, we speak of birth parents as voluntarily choosing to place their children for adoption because they are under no obligation from the State to terminate their parental rights as a result of neglect or abuse. Yet the term voluntary does not reflect the reality of many birth parents who make an adoption plan because of pressure from their partners, families, churches, communities, economic situations, and more. Likewise, adoptive parents may be unduly influenced by situations of infertility, a sense of duty, or pressure from a spouse, while infant adoptees themselves have no choice in the matter of their adoption. The matching process and the use of preference sheets introduce conditions into the adoption process. Birth parents and PAPs, alike, can feel judged and rejected, and some adoptees struggle to live up to the expectations that they perceive their adoptive parents have for their "chosen" child. Finally, human adoption carries with it the possibility of reversals and revocations, as well as actual disruptions of placements and dissolutions of finalized adoptions.

Therefore, Christians who are considering private domestic adoption should favor policies and practices that enable birth parents to make deliberate decisions. Such practices include the provision of adequate and unbiased counseling about alternatives to adoption as well as options within adoption and awareness of resources that may be available to them if they wish to parent their children. Regardless of what a given state may permit, wisdom and compassion should prevail in determining the timeline for the signing of consents in order to protect vulnerable birth mothers, as well as PAPs who have their own emotional and financial investments in the adoption, and the children who can be caught in the middle.

REFLECT AND RESPOND

Read about families who completed private domestic adoptions in appendices 1, 2, 3, and 4.

- What do you consider to be the advantages of adopting an infant? What challenges would this choice present for you?

- In light of what you have learned about independent and agency adoptions, does either approach appeal to you? What do you see as their advantages or disadvantages?

- How important to you is the ability to choose a specific type of child? How comfortable are you with remaining open to whatever God may provide?

- How concerned are you about the cost of adoption? What is a realistic budget for you?

- What is your ideal timeline for adoption? Why?

- How do you feel about the need to reveal all aspects of your life in a home study? Are there any particular areas of concern for you?

4

Domestic Adoption through the State

Jeopardy! Who Wants to Be a Millionaire? Deal or No Deal? At crucial points in each of these game shows, contestants decide whether to risk their potential winnings in hopes of an even greater economic payoff. The daredevil throws caution to the wind for the chance to win (or lose) it all, while the less adventurous contestant passes on the possibility of a big reward in order to take the smaller sure thing.

Many decisions of daily life involve relatively low risk. Should I wear my blue or black slacks? What should we eat for dinner? However, the stakes can be high when it comes to adoption. When our family took placement of an older child from the foster care system, one well-meaning friend bluntly declared, "A teenager is far too risky. After all, children over two are already ruined. This will never work out, and it will break your hearts." Indeed, adoption (particularly public domestic adoption) comes with significant risks.

Public domestic adoptions within the United States involve the permanent placement of children who have spent time within

Domestic Adoption through the State

the nation's child welfare system. The seeds of that system were planted in the late 1800s when private child protection societies sought to intervene on behalf of vulnerable children by relocating them to orphanages or to family-based foster care. Comparable public agencies slowly appeared throughout the twentieth century. Today many individual states have their own public children services agencies (PCSAs), often called child protective services, child welfare agencies, or children service bureaus. Among other duties, PCSAs typically serve as the adoption service providers (ASPs) for public domestic adoptions. In many cases, prospective adoptive parents (PAPs) seeking to adopt through the State are assigned to a particular ASP based on the county or region where they live.

THE WAITING CHILDREN

Children enter State custody through no fault of their own. Rather, they are removed from their parents by judicial order when there is evidence of abuse or neglect, or when their parents are incarcerated, institutionalized, unwilling, or otherwise unable to care for them. The State hopes that biological parents, with the help of services and supports and under the guidance of a structured case plan, can reunify with their children, but the sad reality is that for many children in State care it is never safe to return home. Eventually, parental rights are terminated, and the State seeks adoptive parents for them.

All children who become available for public domestic adoption have spent time within the child welfare system and are coming from foster care. Practically, this means that they have lived with extended family members, or in foster homes, group homes, or child residential centers, and legally they are in the permanent custody of the State. Given their histories, many of the children have special medical, psychological, behavioral, or developmental needs (see chapter 6). The great majority of available children are older or part of a sibling group, and many public adoptions are transracial (see chapter 7).

Thinking about Adoption

According to the U.S. government's Adoption and Foster Care Analysis and Reporting System (AFCARS), in 2014 nearly fifty-one thousand children were adopted through PCSAs. Moreover, of the approximately four hundred fifteen thousand children who remained in foster care that year, nearly one hundred eight thousand were eligible for adoption but had not found permanent placements.

WHAT TO EXPECT WITH A PUBLIC ADOPTION

Many states offer two routes by which PAPs might adopt children who are in State custody. Those who *foster-to-adopt* become licensed foster parents with the hope that foster placements may culminate in adoption. Those who select *adoption-only* do not become foster parents but seek to be matched with children only after the termination of parental rights (TPR) has occurred and the children are legally free to be adopted.

Both foster-to-adopt and adoption-only approaches come with low or no fees for PAPs. In fact, instead of paying fees, PAPs may be compensated. Prior to the finalization of an adoption, PAPs may receive per diem payments for children in their care, and families often receive a monthly adoption stipend even after finalization. Children involved in public adoption may be eligible for Medicaid and other assistance, such as in-state college tuition costs, depending upon the specific state.

Adoption-only

Adoption-only PAPs typically undergo training and complete the home study process with a PCSA before working to identify an appropriate waiting child. You may review child profiles provided by your PCSA or search national websites. Some PCSAs arrange events for PAPs to meet local children who are in need of families. The PCSA that oversees the care of a selected child makes the decision about whether you are a suitable match, and if the child is from

Domestic Adoption through the State

another state, the placement is subject to the Interstate Compact on the Placement of Children (ICPC). As with private adoptions, once a matched child is placed in your home, there is a probationary period requiring postplacement visits before finalization can occur.

Foster-to-Adopt

The foster-to-adopt process is more complex. PAPs first pursue licensing through the local PCSA or other foster care licensing agency by receiving training, clearing background checks, completing a home study, and passing various safety inspections. As with other kinds of adoption, you will specify your preferences concerning the age, race, special needs, gender, and number of children you are prepared to foster and potentially adopt. PAPs assume legal risk when they welcome children for whom parental rights have not been terminated, so despite the many unknowns, some adoption workers further classify placements as high legal risk if they suspect that a child's placement will not be permanent and as low legal risk if they think adoption is the likely outcome. Licensed families then wait to receive calls about children who match their established criteria, and the wait can be long for those who want a young, healthy child with low legal risk. When a call does come, PCSAs may expect you to make a quick decision and to be available immediately.

"Because we already have several children, we are more open to a situation where the outcome is uncertain."
—An adoptive mother (Appendix 9)

Children can come to you directly from birth, immediately upon removal from their family of origin, or after having spent time in one or more foster homes. Yet the fact that these children are in foster care indicates that they have suffered trauma of some kind, whether through abuse or neglect. They may require mental health, substance abuse, and various other services to address the harm they have suffered. Furthermore, every change of placement may cause regression in social, intellectual,

Thinking about Adoption

and behavioral development, and some children endure multiple placement changes. Children in foster care can have difficulty building trust relationships and may even sabotage placements to avoid being let down by yet another adult. In this sense, PAPs face additional risks in their attempts to parent these children.

Foster-to-adopt PAPs act as surrogate parents to children in their homes. Even as emotional bonds may grow, you lack legal standing in the child's life. You must follow state-prescribed orders regarding schooling, medical evaluations, court appearances, family contact, visitations from caseworkers, and mandatory paperwork. Most significantly, the State expects you to assist in their efforts to reunify children with their birth families even if it is your hope to parent the child permanently.

Foster-to-adopt situations move forward in various ways. Biological parents can make adequate progress on their case plans and regain custody of their children. Children may move to a different foster family if you or the PCSA decide that their best interests are not being met in your home. PCSAs may locate an appropriate relative who takes over as the child's temporary or permanent caregiver. If TPR (Termination of Parental Rights) occurs, you may be given the opportunity to adopt your foster child, although PCSAs may consider other possible families. PAPs who are selected as the best match will ultimately be able to finalize the child's adoption.

THE STANDARDS OF THE STATE

Both by statute and by necessity, PCSAs follow specific standards as they seek families for children. Family preservation is a priority, and the reunification of children with biological parents is the goal whenever possible. Any decision to terminate parental rights requires due process, even if it takes several years.

The State also believes that permanency is in a child's best interest. Following TPR, PCSAs want children to be adopted as quickly as possible. For that reason, PCSAs may engage in concurrent planning, whereby they simultaneously work toward a child's reunification with the family of origin while also developing an

> "I was concerned because the county emphasized reunification of children with their biological parents. I feared going through a disrupted placement, but I figured we would accept only highly adoptable placements in order to minimize the risk."
> —An adoptive mother (Appendix 9)

adoption plan. When children are placed with PAPs as part of concurrent planning, PAPs accept legal risk.

Finally, in all matching decisions, kinship care is favored over placement with non-relatives. This means that non-relative PAPs, even those who have been involved in the care of a child as part of concurrent planning, may not be selected to adopt a child particularly if a suitable caregiver can be identified from among the members of the child's biological family.

IS PUBLIC DOMESTIC ADOPTION A GOOD FIT FOR ME?

PAPs who are concerned about the financial cost of adoption will find that public adoptions are very affordable. Either type of public domestic adoption can be a good fit if you are able to parent an older child or a sibling group. You are particularly well-suited if you have the personal and community resources that would enable you to address a history of abuse or neglect, if you are comfortable with a process that can be highly unpredictable, and if you have patience for paperwork and bureaucracy. PAPs who adopt through the State should be willing to interact with birth families, either as foster parents, or by virtue of the fact that even after adoption many children maintain ties with siblings or other extended family members. PAPs who are not open to a child with special needs will find few potential matches in public domestic adoption.

Those who have any previous experience with the foster care system or who can envision themselves being a positive influence in the life of a child, even if it is only temporary, may be most comfortable becoming foster-to-adopt parents, knowing that the outcome is uncertain. It can be a path for PAPs looking for a younger child or a quicker placement, and it may give you an advantage over adoption-only families in the matching process. Due to the emotional risk, foster-to-adopt is not recommended for PAPs who have lost children or who are seeking to become first-time parents. The adoption-only route will appeal to PAPs desiring the security of knowing that the children placed with them are already available for adoption. However, the wait for a match can be long when you are competing with kin or foster parents who have an established connection with a child.

> "Multiple prior generations in my family had even been foster parents. But I thought I was not strong enough to handle the anguish and heartache of loving children and then having to let them go especially after having had miscarriages."
> — An adoptive mother (Appendix 10)

THEOLOGICAL CONSIDERATIONS

The United States is not the first government to enact regulations and policies related to the care of children. Among the laws that God provides for the ancient Hebrews as they organize themselves into a fledgling theocracy are those that govern the attitudes and interactions of the community regarding the most vulnerable in their midst. The community's compassion toward and provision for the fatherless are to reflect the character of God (Pss 68:5, 146:9). Although the adoption of children is nowhere commanded, God establishes a system intent on caring for the fatherless (Deut 14:28–29; 24:19–22; 26:12–13) and explicitly including them in Israel's communal life (Deut 16:11, 14).

Despite the fact that the United States is not a theocracy, Christian involvement in the child welfare system today, whether through foster care or adoption, is certainly consistent with God's desire for his people to tend to vulnerable children who live in their own communities. However, those who select public domestic adoption must cooperate with the State and abide by its decisions

Domestic Adoption through the State

about child placement. Although it can be difficult, God's people are to recognize and submit to God-given authority, even that of a secular government (Rom 13:1).

The degree to which the State prioritizes reunification of children with their biological families, for instance, sometimes creates tension for PAPs who desire to adopt. Even if you believe your family could provide a better permanent home for a foster child in your care, it is a matter of integrity and Christian witness that you do all you can to nurture, rather than sabotage, reunification. In fact, such priorities align with God's own interest in forgiveness and restoration (Matt 18:21–22, Luke 23:34, Acts 5:30–31, Eph 1:7–10). PAPs who are unable to act accordingly would do well to pursue a different path to adoption.

> "Ultimately it was clear that we were really at cross purposes with the county. We appreciated their push to reunify families, but we wanted permanency, so after a year and a half, we reconsidered our approach."
> —Adoptive parents (Appendix 3)

REFLECT AND RESPOND

Read about families who completed public domestic adoptions in appendices 9 and 10.

- What is the biggest risk you have ever taken? Are you inclined to be a risk-taker, or are you more risk-averse? Are you more comfortable with certain kinds of risks (emotional, financial, physical, etc.) than others?

Thinking about Adoption

- What do you see as the challenges of adopting a child who has experienced trauma? Are there ways that you feel prepared to address these challenges?

- In light of what you have learned about foster-to-adopt and adoption-only through the State, does either approach appeal to you? What do you see as the advantages or disadvantages of each process?

- Various websites such as adoptuskids.org and heartgallery ofamerica.org provide a photo listing of some of the many children who are available to be adopted from foster care. Take some time to look through the child profiles, keeping in mind that sensitive information about each child's background and needs is not presented to the general public. From the little information that you can access, reflect on what you have learned about the waiting children.

5

Intercountry Adoption

Mexico. Venezuela. Italy. Scotland. Ukraine. Bosnia and Herzegovina. Our passports document these and many other places that we have visited through our love of travel and our desire to learn about other people and cultures. Our home displays a handful of particularly meaningful mementos from around the world. Sitting on our bookshelf is a twenty-five millimeter brass shell casing from Sarajevo, a relic of the ethnic, religious, and political conflict that engulfed the Balkans in the years following the breakup of Yugoslavia. An enterprising craftsman hammered intricate designs into the brass, transforming it into a piece of art. To us, this particular piece symbolizes the complex ways that people and nations experience tragedy, seize opportunities, and find the good. We see similar complexities when it comes to intercountry adoption.

Intercountry adoption (ICA), also called international adoption, involves the adoption of children who have been born in a foreign country. American interest in ICA began following World War II as news about the needs of orphans around the world spread. ICA attracted even more PAPs when the number of infants available for domestic adoption waned. The practice faced early

Thinking about Adoption

opposition from those who disliked the interracial families that ICA often produced, while today some denounce it as a tool of western colonialism. Tragically, a lack of regulation and oversight has allowed the unscrupulous to exploit parents, kidnap children, and profit from human trafficking under the guise of ICA.

THE HAGUE CONVENTION

The development of the Hague Convention on the Protection of Children and Co-operation in Respect of Inter-Country Adoption in 1993 stands as a significant milestone with regard to the transnational regulation of ICA. The United States implemented Convention guidelines in 2008, and currently nearly one hundred countries are party to the Convention. Among other safeguards, designated central authorities in each Convention country must establish that children are truly eligible for adoption, that proper consents are in place, and that fees are disclosed and regulated. They preserve known information about the child's history and match children with suitable foreign PAPs only when they cannot secure permanent domestic caregivers. Nevertheless, the system is imperfect. Convention guidelines have minimized but not eliminated abuses. Yet they also have increased costs and extended the adoption process, which exposes waiting children to the damaging effects of institutionalization for greater periods of time.

SELECTING A COUNTRY

The United States government permits Americans to adopt children from many Convention and some non-Convention countries. China, Ethiopia, and Ukraine have been popular countries for American families in recent years, but the landscape of ICA changes frequently. Nations can and do close their international adoption programs with little warning, and countries that once placed healthy infants now may limit their international referrals primarily to children with various special needs.

Intercountry Adoption

If you discern a calling to ICA, your own background, travels, or love of a certain culture may draw you immediately to one country or region. Yet each country sets its own requirements for PAPs with regard to age, marital status, health, income, family size, and more. If you are twenty-eight years old or have been married just one year, you are not eligible to adopt from China even if you have trekked the entire Great Wall or are fluent in Mandarin! The United States Department of State website provides up-to-date information for each country.

Your selection of a country and your choice of an ASP are best made concurrently. It will not do to have your heart set on adopting from Haiti if your preferred ASP does not have an active Haitian adoption program. Good ASPs will also help you to evaluate international programs since countries differ greatly in the age, gender, and health of available children. There are also significant differences between countries in the average time that it takes for approved PAPs to receive a referral for a child, the particular residency requirements that stipulate how many trips are necessary, the duration of the stay in country, and whether both members of a married couple must travel.

Factors to ponder as you compare ASPs include how long a particular ASP has been working in your chosen country, their involvement in broader humanitarian efforts in that locale, and whether they have actual staff members abroad. Learn whether you would travel independently or in a group to pick up children, who arranges travel and accommodations, and whether the ASP provides translators, medical professionals, and others to assist while you are abroad. Obtain a full disclosure of expected fees, and clarify what happens if something should cause your program to close after you begin. Finally, recent regulations require all ASPs who engage in defined ICA services to have federal

> "We searched online for Christian adoption agencies, and chose one with a good record and a commitment to broader ministries in the countries where they worked."
> —An adoptive father (Appendix 6)

Thinking about Adoption

accreditation or approval or to work under a primary provider who does. Consult the United State Department of State's Adoption Service Provider Search webpage to confirm the status of an ASP.

WHAT TO EXPECT WITH AN INTERCOUNTRY ADOPTION

To some degree the actual ICA process depends upon whether you adopt from a Convention country or a non-Convention country, but typical steps include a home study, immigration pre-approval, adoption dossier, referral, legal proceedings in the country of origin, visa application, and possible finalization and post-adoption reports. There is a mountain of paperwork to climb to satisfy state, federal, foreign, and international laws!

A home study for ICA must meet any requirements of your state of residence plus those of the United States Citizenship and Immigration Services (USCIS), your selected foreign country, and perhaps the Convention. In some cases very specific sections and wording are necessary. For this reason, you should determine the country from which you seek to adopt before beginning your home study.

With a completed home study, you can apply for USCIS pre-approval to adopt from your selected country. The precise form and timeline for submission differs for Convention and non-Convention countries. Home study updates may be needed if the document is not submitted to USCIS in a timely manner or if there is a significant change in your household.

The packet of information used to present PAPs to foreign officials is called an *adoption dossier*. Each country dictates the contents of the dossier, but be prepared to submit originals of your home study, birth certificates, medical reports, financial information, proof of immigration pre-approval, and a copy of your passport, in addition to any country-specific forms. Often paperwork must be both notarized and apostilled, a process by which the Secretary of State further authenticates a document. It is possible

Intercountry Adoption

to compile your dossier yourself, but many PAPs seek professional help so that no errors or omissions cause delays.

After processing your dossier, the foreign country refers a particular child as a match for you. You typically receive a child profile, which includes a photo and known medical and background information. Although seeing your potential son or daughter can stir a deep emotional response, take all the permitted time to consider prayerfully and review carefully the information. Consult with doctors and professionals who specialize in international adoption before accepting the referral.

Once you accept a referral, you await clearance to travel to your child's country of origin, or in some cases, to arrange for an escort to bring your child to the United States. International travel is stressful and expensive, and the sights, sounds, smells, and tastes you encounter will feel unfamiliar. That said, any time that you have abroad is a valuable opportunity to see the world through your child's eyes, explore the culture of your child's homeland, and possibly connect with those who have been your child's caregivers and peers. Cherish these days, and preserve these memories for you and your child.

While overseas PAPs follow the local legal system to complete a full and final adoption on site or to secure a transfer of guardianship, which frees the child to leave the country with you. Permission to transport your child into the United States requires you to work with the U.S. Embassy or Consulate overseas in order to obtain the appropriate visa.

After you and your child return home, take advantage of all available post-adoption services to help with the transition, which can be difficult for everyone. Your ASP will assist you if your country requires post-adoption reports at regular intervals to document that the child is receiving proper care and adjusting appropriately. Legally you may need to finalize the adoption in front of a judge in your state, but in accordance with the Child Citizen Act of 2000, very few adoptees will need to complete a separate application to gain citizenship.

Thinking about Adoption

IS INTERCOUNTRY ADOPTION A GOOD FIT FOR ME?

ICA may appeal to PAPs who wish to avoid the uncertainty of the domestic adoption process. ICA follows relatively predictable steps even though the timeline can be variable. There is no wondering if or when you will be chosen by a birth mother, and all children who are referred have already been legally declared to be available for adoption so there is minimal risk that you will be left empty-handed at the end. Although costs can easily range from $15,000 to $50,000 or more, most fees are clearly outlined at the outset.

ICA may be a good fit for PAPs who think their chances of being chosen by a birth mother are slim, who are willing to have little or no contact with the child's family of origin, and who are prepared to live with unanswered questions about the adoptee's genetic, medical, and social background. It is best to be flexible concerning the age, race, and health of the adoptee. ICA is ill-advised for PAPs who wish to adopt an infant or who would reject a child with special physical, emotional, or developmental needs. Finally, those who do not wish to travel internationally or who would be unable to stay overseas for an extended amount of time could struggle with ICA.

> "We were attracted to intercountry adoption because we felt like the need of an orphan overseas was probably greater than that of a child in the United States, and we wanted to avoid the risk of having a failed placement."
> —An adoptive mother (Appendix 6)

> "International adoption also just did not appeal to me. The travel would have used up all of my vacation time from work and left me unable to have any time to be home with the baby once we returned stateside. Plus I am just not very flexible when it comes to foreign environments."
> —An adoptive father (Appendix 5)

Intercountry Adoption

THEOLOGICAL CONSIDERATIONS

Multiple biblical teachings support the concept of ICA. Jesus' memorable parable about a Good Samaritan makes it clear that Christian love for neighbor extends beyond the house next door (Luke 10:25-37). Paul connects the idea of joining God's household with acquiring new citizenship (Eph 2:19). Indeed, God himself crossed far more than national boundaries when he came from heaven to earth to make a way for the adoption of his children (Gal 4:4-5).

Yet the ethical landmines associated with the actual practice of ICA call for caution, so that as we walk in love (Eph 5:2), we also walk in light (Eph 5:8-17). The apostle Paul illustrates the sort of wisdom that might be appropriate when he offers parameters for the care of widows. While 1 Timothy 5:3-16 does not directly discuss orphans, the parallels between orphans and widows are plentiful. Indeed, Scripture habitually speaks of both in the same breath (Exod 22:22; Deut 10:18; 24:17, 19-21; 27:19; Pss 68:5; 94:6; 146:9; Isa 1:17; Jer 22:3; Ezek 22:7; Zech 7:10; Mal 3:5; Jas 1:27).

Paul explains that the task of caring for a widow falls first to her extended family members (1 Tim 5:4, 16). Only when a widow has no family does the local church community intervene. In similar fashion, we should not promote ICA as the first response to the global orphan crisis. Whenever possible, Christians should favor policies and practices that enable living parents to raise their children, that encourage kinship placements, or that give local Christians the ability to minister to the needy in their own communities. ICA stands in the gap only for those children who are truly orphans with no other hope of personal care and permanent support.

Additionally, Paul discourages the church from establishing formal, permanent relationships with widows when doing so provides temptations and opportunities for sin (1 Tim 5:11-14). In like manner, it may be that Christian PAPs should choose not to adopt from nations when doing so promotes the commoditization of children. There is a strong likelihood of foul play when a country seems able to supply numerous young and healthy children quickly in response to foreign demand for ICA.

Although the unilateral relocation of significant numbers of children from places of great poverty to those of great wealth has allowed for horrific abuses, ICA nonetheless offers a great gift to some of the neediest children in the world who have no other hope of family or even of survival. When done with caution, ICA is a beautiful testimony to the power of Christ to tear down barriers and make peace.

REFLECT AND RESPOND

Read about families who completed intercountry adoptions in appendices 6, 7, and 8.

- Do you have ethical concerns regarding intercountry adoption? What steps might you take to address these?

- Describe the sort of child you envisioned as the typical international adoptee before reading this chapter. In light of what you have read, has that picture changed? In what way(s)?

Intercountry Adoption

- When you consider intercountry adoption, are you drawn to any particular countries? Which ones? Why?

- What do you see as the advantages and disadvantages of intercountry adoption for your family?

6

Special Needs Adoption

Every now and then we enjoy watching the award-wining PBS show *Antiques Roadshow*. On the program, people present their potential treasures to appraisers, who analyze them and reveal their assessment. At times the experts explain how a similar item, in pristine condition, is worth a great deal of money, but then they reveal how some small variation like a missing button or a faded color on the particular item reduces its value to a mere fraction. It may long remain a beloved piece with sentimental value to its owners, but the apparent imperfection renders it undesirable or nearly worthless at auction.

Sadly, our society assigns value to people in accordance with prevailing cultural standards and perceived excellence or shortcomings. Adoption, regrettably, can magnify such injustice. In the past century, Americans tended to view adoption as a means of providing the ideal parents with the perfect child. The healthy, white infant emerged as the preferred adoptee, while the white, middle-class, two-parent family with a young stay-at-home mom and a bread-winning dad constituted the model adoptive parents. In contrast, children with disabilities were considered to be defective and unadoptable. They and other less desirables could languish

Special Needs Adoption

for years without forever families, while couples who were older, single applicants, and others who did not fit the mold, were rarely approved to adopt.

As adoption became more child-centered, ASPs began to redefine their task in terms of finding parents for waiting children. Some concluded that difficult-to-place children warranted exceptional placements if they were ever to find permanent homes, and they initiated adoption programs allowing singles to adopt them. They reasoned that it might be better for a child to have one parent rather than none. Today PAPs who are willing to adopt hard-to-place children face fewer restrictions with regard to their age, marital status, number of children, etc., and they often find incentives such as minimal fees and relatively quick placements. In some instances, children are also eligible for ongoing subsidies, Medicaid, and free or reduced-cost post-adoptive services.

Since the late 1960s, various domestic agencies have emerged that actively promote what are now called *special needs* adoptions. In the context of adoption, the special needs umbrella covers an incredibly diverse range of circumstances and can include children who are older; have physical, mental, emotional, or behavioral challenges; belong to a racial minority (see chapter 7); and/or are part of a sibling group of two or more that wishes to remain together. The majority of these children are in State custody, but children adopted internationally increasingly come with special needs as more countries seek to place healthy babies with their own citizens.

A SPECIAL CALLING?

It is quite possible that you do not feel prepared to pursue special needs adoption in an intentional way. Do not decide to do so out of pressure or guilt. Nonetheless, remember that no path to adoption guarantees the health and well-being of the adoptee. Children who are adopted as healthy infants with no known risk factors may come to manifest some sort of special need over time. Some studies even suggest that adopted children in general develop

Thinking about Adoption

behavioral problems (ADD/ADHD, anxiety, etc.) at a rate higher than the general population, although others dispute these findings. All PAPs would do well to think about and be prepared for the possibility of special needs.

Parenting is not easy even in the best of circumstances. To be a parent is to expect sleepless nights, sniffling noses, and stinky bottoms. There will be broken bones, broken windows, and broken hearts. For various reasons, the challenges are often magnified for families formed through special needs adoptions. PAPs must prepare wisely and also make plans for post-adoptive assistance.

> "We were not intentionally seeking a child who was going to have long-term special needs, although if it turned out that way, that would be okay."
> —An adoptive mother
> (Appendix 5)

One way to prepare is to consider how your own gifts, strengths, and life experiences might work to the benefit of any particular children you might parent. PAPs who are highly compassionate, patient, and not easily discouraged, as well as those who have been foster parents previously, may do well with many kinds of special needs adoptions. Yet caring for a medically needy child calls for a different skill set than nurturing a child with oppositional defiant disorder. The PAP who does well with a sibling group of three older children could struggle with a child who has post-traumatic stress disorder.

Consider any experience that you may have with a particular disability or medical diagnosis. A PAP with a hearing impairment and the ability to speak in sign language may choose to adopt a deaf child. A physical therapist might be well-suited to parent a child with low muscle tone. The mom with dyslexia might relate well to a child with a mild learning disability. Even the older couple who has already raised several children may find that they can more easily step into a parenting role with an older adoptee.

On the contrary, certain life circumstances render some PAPs ill-prepared for special needs adoption. If you lack flexibility with your work schedule, would have a difficult time with a child who

Special Needs Adoption

needs frequent medical appointments or therapy sessions, or are unable to replace your two-seater car with something larger, then your family would be hard-pressed to accommodate a sibling group of four.

Preparation involves taking great care in considering the circumstances of a particular child before committing to a match. Seek complete information about the child's diagnosis, prognosis, and both past and current treatments. Evaluate the cause of the special need, its intensity, how treatable it is, and whether effects are likely to be temporary or lifelong. While adoption workers in the United States are required to disclose any documented details, keep in mind that there may be things that are unknown. Birth parents do not always provide a full and accurate background, and paperwork is not always filed properly. For children born outside of the United States, there are often holes in their history, and facts may remain undisclosed as a result of differing cultural practices or poorly translated documents. Increasingly PAPs who adopt internationally do not learn about the existence or full extent of a special need until after the child's placement.

Take the time to review any details you do receive with trained medical or psychological practitioners. These professionals can help you to create realistic expectations for the future. For instance, it is possible that the toddler with a heart defect will undergo numerous surgeries over several years and then experience no long-term problems. The non-ambulatory child might never walk, yet could anticipate a life of independence. Victims of trauma may learn to regulate and manage their emotional and behavioral issues when given the appropriate tools. Other children with severe medical or emotional conditions will require lifelong care with little to no prospect of improvement or independence. Preparation invites caregivers to consider all of these factors both prayerfully and logically.

Children who come via special needs adoption generally require specialized services for education, ongoing counseling and therapy, or regular and complicated medical services. PAPs should expect to be (or become) competent in maneuvering the healthcare and/or educational systems in order to advocate for their child. Adoptive parents themselves benefit from ongoing training about parenting, respite care, counseling, and family preservation services. Find out whether these services and supports are widely available where you live, what is needed for you to access them, and how you will pay for them.

Finally, plan to develop a strong network for social support. Will family members assist you with child care? Can you receive encouragement from a friend or a church ministry that provides dinner or a respite night once a month? You may find emotional support and practical advice by connecting with other local families who have adopted children with special needs or by joining online support groups for families like yours.

THEOLOGICAL CONSIDERATIONS

All people are infinitely valuable because God is our Creator (Col 1:16). Specifically, God has created all human beings as his image-bearers and as the pinnacle of creation (Gen 1:27–28; Matt 6:26). He knits individuals together in the womb (Ps 139:13–14), even those with disabilities (Exod 4:11). Whereas the world seeks to honor those who are attractive, athletic, powerful, intelligent, or rich, God's perspective is profoundly different. In God's economy, the weak are strong, the foolish shame the wise (1 Cor 1:27), and the heart supersedes the appearance (1 Sam 16:7).

Since God values all people, the people of God also should hold all

> "We went in wanting to adopt a healthy child. We remember thinking that it is sweet that people adopt special needs kids, but that is not our family. But after a conversation in which an agency worker explained that the wait for healthy children was significantly longer, we felt burdened. We questioned why we would get in a long line of people waiting for a healthy child if our heart for adoption was to minister and meet a need."
>
> —An adoptive mother (Appendix 7)

Special Needs Adoption

human life as sacred. Christian PAPs can approach special needs adoption as an invitation to see through God's eyes, embrace those whom the world considers to be outcasts, and shower them with love and honor in service of our Lord Jesus (Matt 25:34–40). The daily trials will challenge you to seek God as the one who provides for every need (Phil 4:19), and life may not be pretty. However, those who discern that God has genuinely called them to special needs adoption can find encouragement in the example of Christ, who himself endured great humiliation and costly sacrifice for our benefit and for God's glory (Phil 2:1–11).

REFLECT AND RESPOND

Read about families who completed special needs adoptions in appendices 7, 8, 9, and 10.

- Reflect on your own personality and character qualities with regard to love, empathy, flexibility, peace, patience, kindness, and gentleness. Which ones are areas of strength for you? Which ones are weaknesses?

- What scares you and what interests you about special needs adoption? Record your thoughts with regard to each category below.
    - an older child

- a sibling group

- a medically needy child

- a child with emotional/behavioral issues

- Do you have training or experiences in a specific area that could help you to parent a child with a particular kind of special need? Do you have any life circumstances that would make it difficult or unwise for you to adopt a child with special needs?

- How accessible are services that could assist you in parenting a child with medical needs? With emotional/behavioral disorders?

Special Needs Adoption

- Describe your support system of friends and family. In what ways could they assist as you parent a child with special needs?

- Do you think God might be calling you to special needs adoption? Why, or why not?

7

Transracial Adoption

Our own family could fill a book if we tried to list all of the physical similarities and differences that exist among the four of us. All of us have ten fingers and ten toes. Three have brown eyes. Two have black hair. Each one has a unique skin color: tan, peach, chocolate, and olive. Clearly ours is an interracial family, and it came about in part through transracial adoption.

Transracial adoption (TRA), also called interracial adoption, refers to adoptions in which one or both of the adoptive parents do not share the same racial identity as the child. Although we use the terms interchangeably, certain adoption contexts may prefer one term over the other. Discussing interracial adoption is tricky since the concept of race itself is a social construct built upon an intersection of factors related to biology, ethnicity, culture, national background, and more. There are many strong arguments for viewing skin color as a poor means of defining race, but when it comes to transracial adoption, concerns about skin color dominate the conversation. Quite simply, this most visible component of interracial adoption creates conspicuous families in a way that same-race adoptions do not.

Transracial Adoption

TRA may occur either domestically or internationally, and the adoption process itself does not differ significantly from that which occurs in their same-race counterparts. Unique elements might include a requirement for prospective adoptive parents (PAPs) to complete training with regard to race and culture and the inclusion of an explicit statement in the home study regarding the family's interest in and approval for a transracial adoption. In some instances, families who choose domestic adoption of an African-American or mixed-race child may also find a reduction in the fee charged by an adoption agency, a shorter waiting period to be matched with a child, or greater flexibility with regard to such things as the age and marital status requirements to qualify as a prospective parent.

IT IS NOT ALL BLACK AND WHITE

Historically in the American context, TRA has most frequently involved white parents and non-white children. Exceptions occur on occasion but are often fraught with additional difficulties. Increases in TRA have coincided with the availability of reliable birth control, the legalization of abortion, and the social shift toward acceptance of unmarried mothers, all of which have contributed to fewer healthy, white infants being placed for adoption. The increasing presence of interracial couples and families in society in general, as well as the growing popularity of intercountry adoption, also has prompted more families to consider adopting across racial lines.

In general there are three separate categories of attitudes and practices regarding TRA in the United States: transracial adoption of black children, transracial adoption of

> "Our families are from the South, and while they supported our interracial adoptions in theory, there are issues. They love our children, but they say inappropriate things about other black people or about racial issues in the news, so we cannot always be around them." —An adoptive mother (Appendix 2)

Thinking about Adoption

Native American children, and transracial adoption of children of other races. Beginning with the first documented placement of a black child with white parents in 1948, only about 12,000 similar placements occurred in total through 1975, and the practice faced opposition from several fronts. Some states retained bans on TRA even after the 1967 Supreme Court ruling that laws prohibiting interracial marriage were unconstitutional. In 1972, the National Association of Black Social Workers argued that a black child could not develop in a healthy manner without having black parents, although outcome studies have not upheld this claim. The 1973 adoption guidelines by the Child Welfare League of America maintained that same-race placements were always preferable. It was not until the 1996 amendment to the Multiethnic Placement Act (MEPA) that adoption agencies receiving federal funding were prohibited from routinely using race, color, or national origin as the sole factor to deny or delay the placement of children. Nonetheless, MEPA allows agencies to consider race as one of the many factors that influence placement decisions, and some adoption agencies may have a preference for race matching whenever possible.

The adoption of Native American children stands as a significant exception to MEPA, and there are special adoption laws unique to this population. The Indian Adoption Project (1958–1967) placed 395 native children in white families. Although studies found the children and families overall to be well-adjusted, the project faced significant Native American pushback. Some Native American leaders accused it of being akin to ethnic genocide. The result was the 1978 Indian Child Welfare Act, which made it virtually impossible for anyone without tribal affiliation to adopt Native American children.

Social attitudes are significantly more accepting of the placement of children of other races; particularly when the children are adopted internationally, which is often the case. Quite simply, American culture does not have the same long national history of racial conflict with people of Asian, Latin American, or Eastern European descent.

THEOLOGICAL CONSIDERATIONS

The Bible does not address race directly in the way that it is commonly spoken of today. The most similar category that appears is that of ethnicity, which speaks of people groups who may share social, cultural, and/or national identities. It does not single out the matter of skin color, although people from distinct ethnic groups might differ from one another in this regard.

Scripture repeatedly reveals God's intention to create a family that includes people from all ethnic groups and incorporates people of all races. For instance, Abram was called into relationship with God so that "all peoples" might receive God's blessing (Gen 12:1–3). The resurrected Jesus instructs his followers to make disciples of all people groups (Matt 28:18–20). Finally, the book of Revelation records praise to God for redeeming people "from every tribe and language and people and nation" (Rev 5:9). There can be no doubt that the family of God is multiracial.

God is glorified and his people are blessed when human relationships and earthly institutions reflect the principles that God has established for his kingdom. This is seen when Jesus teaches his disciples to pray: "Your kingdom come, your will be done on earth as it is in heaven" (Matt 6:10). Since it is God's will for the family of God to cross races and ethnicities, it cannot be counter to his will for human families to do the same.

Interracial couples, interracial families, and individuals who identify as multiracial are becoming increasingly common. Nonetheless, interracial families, particularly those that are a result of adoption, remain somewhat rare in specific locales. In public contexts such as the local restaurant or the parent pick-up line at school, a family formed by TRA is a living billboard for adoption and racial harmony. Just like the multiethnic church, interracial families stand as a prophetic object lesson of the new kingdom reality for those who are in Christ, but because such reconciliation

Thinking about Adoption

and fellowship is not the norm, it often attracts attention from the sympathetic and encouraging, the antagonistic and rude, and the simply curious.

Supporters of TRA may see it as a victory for civil rights and racial reconciliation, and they recognize that the practice facilitates the placement of children who might otherwise go without families and permanent homes for long periods of time. Objectors to TRA believe that adoptive parents will be unable to meet the child's physical, emotional, and social needs in adequate ways because a white mother will not know how to care for her black daughter's hair, or a non-minority father will be unable to prepare his tan son to navigate a complicated American racial landscape. They suggest that the child will struggle to develop a healthy self-identity since she will lack immediate role models of her own race, and she will be deprived of full access to her own culture. They also maintain that society will ostracize the child, present him with confusing stereotypes and prejudices, and perceive and treat him in ways that may differ markedly from his own self-perception.

None of the objections to TRA are insurmountable, but they stand as a reminder that those who choose to form a family by TRA will need to be characterized by intentionality, openness, and learning with regard to race. Parents intentionally can provide their child with access to same-race friendships and role models or mentors through various life experiences, books, television shows, and personal relationships. They can maintain open and honest communication about privilege and prejudice and actively fight racism together with their child. They can learn what is needed for proper hair and skin care; learn to speak the child's language of origin;

> "We were open to TRA from the outset, but it was one of the things we researched the most once we were in the process. We were shocked to read that some people think it is harmful for the black community and for the child. We did not want to harm a child, so we had to ponder that."
> —An adoptive father (Appendix 4)

and incorporate the music, food, and traditions from the child's racial background into their own practices. Parents should learn what they can about the child's own racial identity and societal perceptions of it, but they should also acknowledge that they cannot learn everything and will need to draw on outside resources who can fill in the gaps and help their child more fully understand what it is like to live as a member of a particular racial community.

Race will not be the sole issue, but it will be an undercurrent that will play out in various ways throughout the child's upbringing. For this reason, families who choose TRA should expect to raise their child in a manner that takes into consideration the unique needs of each child, recognizing that this will include the larger topic of race.

REFLECT AND RESPOND

Read about families who engaged in transracial adoption in appendices 1, 2, 4, 6, 7, 8, and 9.

- With what race(s) do you self-identify? Why? In what ways do you experience racial privilege and/or racial discrimination?

- How easy or difficult do you think it would be for you to parent a child who looks significantly different from you and to have people consider your family to be different? Why?

Thinking about Adoption

- Research the racial composition of your community using census data, the website for your local public school, etc. and complete the chart below.

Racial Category	Percentage of the Population	I interact with people from this population _____. (never or almost never, occasionally, frequently but with little depth, frequently and in meaningful relationships)	It would be _____ (very difficult, moderately difficult, moderately easy, very easy) for me to develop frequent and meaningful relationships with people from this population.	Common stereotypes (positive or negative) that I have heard about people from this population include:

Transracial Adoption

- If you pursue TRA, would your child be visually/culturally isolated in your community? If so, how willing or able are you to move to a more racially diverse area?

- Complete an exercise in which you intentionally put yourself in settings where you are the racial minority. You might seek out shops, restaurants, beauty parlors, social events, or places of worship. Describe your experiences and your feelings. Would you be willing to frequent places/activities like these if you adopt transracially?

- Read the following Bible passages: Genesis 3:20; Acts 15:5–14; Ephesians 2:11–22. List any additional insights that you gain about God's perspective on race and race relations.

Thinking about Adoption

- Engage in open conversations with your family members and friends whom you expect to be part of your support structure as you adopt and parent your child. How do they respond to the idea of interracial adoption? Specific races? What concerns do they have? What resources can they provide?

- Could TRA be a fit for your family? Why might you consider it or reject it?

8

Openness

A man with amnesia awakens in strange circumstances and must follow clues to uncover who he is (*The Bourne Identity*, 2002). An accident erases recent years from the mind of a newly married woman, leaving her to rediscover whom and what she loves (*The Vow*, 2012). Hollywood's memory-loss trope both entertains and challenges audiences with characters who search for their true identities and loved ones. When done well, these stories depict the confusion and anxiety that accompany an individual's struggle to answer "Who am I really?" Sadly, life imitates art for those adoptees who face unanswered questions about their identity and background, and some find the holes in their stories to be the cause of great anguish.

Adoption practices regarding confidentiality, anonymity, and access to records have varied throughout history. Although it was not the case from the beginning, during much of the twentieth century, adoptive placements were shrouded in secrecy. There was no ongoing contact between birth and adoptive families. Adoptive families followed the "as if" principle by trying to live as if they were biological families. Adoptive parents often concealed adoption from their children until adulthood, and in extreme cases, for their entire lives. State laws sealed adoption records completely, even from adoptees themselves.

Such practices intended to protect and benefit everyone involved. Birth parents could go forward and live lives free from shame. Adoptees avoided labels of illegitimacy and painful revelations about their origin. They could bond and live in the stability of the adoptive family without confusion. Adoptive parents did not have to speak of infertility, and they had little fear that the child would reject them or that a birth parent might appear and want the child back.

The 1970s marked a turning point as increasing numbers of adult adoptees made valid demands for their medical, genetic, and social histories, and birth mothers who felt hurt by current practices began to tell their stories more publicly. Since then state laws have been changing in favor of allowing interested parties to gain access to adoption records. Adoption registries emerged to assist adult adoptees and birth families with making connections. Today the general mindset among adoption service providers (ASPs) is one that favors some degree of openness.

AN OPEN INVITATION?

The concept of openness in adoption speaks to the information that is shared and the relationship that exists between the members of the adoption triad before, during, and after an adoption. Birth families and adoptive families, including adoptees themselves, may interact with one another in a wide variety of ways when it comes to how many personal details they disclose and the amount and kinds of contact they maintain. The terms closed, open, and semi-open attempt to categorize this aspect of adoption.

A *closed*, or confidential, adoption is one in which the parties share no identifying information and have no contact with one another, although assisting ASPs may be able to relay some non-identifying background information during the matching process.

In contrast, an *open* adoption includes the exchange of identifying information and direct contact. Birth parents can actively

Openness

select the adoptive family and meet them before placement, sometimes even allowing them to attend the child's birth. In some cases the family of origin and the adoptive family even choose to function more like an extended family! A document called an adoption contract can be written to outline preferences regarding the frequency and means of contact, whether by regular letters, social media accounts, shared photos, phone calls, and/or face-to-face visits. After finalization, however, adoptive parents cannot lose their child for violating the agreement, and they cannot be compelled to maintain contact except in select states where adoption agreements are legally enforceable.

> "All we know about her background is that she was dropped in front of a hospital when she was a week old."
> —An adoptive father
> (Appendix 7)

Semi-open, or mediated, adoptions land somewhere between closed and open adoptions. Parties share non-identifying information and agree to indirect contact that is mediated by the ASP. Again, great flexibility exists regarding the particulars of these arrangements, and a written adoption contract can outline the desires and boundaries. Many PAPs agree to send a letter and photo of the child to the ASP every three months during the first year, every six months during the second year, and annually thereafter until age eighteen.

Proponents of openness believe that birth mothers with open adoptions experience less grief and guilt following placement because they have taken more control over the choice to relinquish and because ongoing interaction allows them to reaffirm the love and care that they have for the child. Such arrangements also help birth families to avoid fantasizing about the child's life because they have actual information and assurances that the child is doing well.

> "We like that our birth parents do not have to look at every child at the mall and wonder if it is their child. They know the children are happy and healthy."
> —An adoptive father
> (Appendix 3)

67

Similarly, open adoptions may minimize adoptees' emotional struggles with loss, grief, abandonment, trust, and identity, particularly if they are able to understand why their birth parents placed them for adoption. Ongoing contact enables adoptees to develop a more realistic picture of the life they might have with their birth family. Later in life they do not face decisions about whether to search for their biological family and risk failure or rejection. And they benefit very concretely from any access to their genetic information and medical history.

Adoptive parents may find that open and semi-open adoptions offer a greater opportunity to show love to members of the birth family and honor their place of significance in an adoptee's life. Regular post-adoptive contact can alleviate fears that birth parents regret the relinquishment as they affirm the adoptive parents' roles in the child's life. Also, having information and contact empowers adoptive parents to support their children's search for answers that will validate them in their dual identity.

Open arrangements do present challenges not unlike those faced by blended families. Each relationship with a birth mother, father, grandparent, or sibling requires unique parameters: someone desires to increase or decrease contact, but parties cannot reach consensus; an adoptive parent fails to provide promised pictures and letters; an adoptee sends questions to a birth parent but receives no response; birth parents share details that cause heartache and grief. Adoptive parents must monitor carefully what sort of contact is in the child's best interest, and when and how to hand over the decision-making to adoptees themselves.

Private domestic adoptions offer a good route for prospective adoptive parents (PAPs) who seek open adoptions because currently most birth mothers request some post-adoptive contact. Since most international adoptions are essentially closed, PAPs who seek closed adoptions may prefer to look overseas rather than facing the prospect of a lengthy wait for a domestic match. PAPs who adopt through the State must follow any court dictates that limit or prohibit interaction with members of the biological family, although older adoptees are frequently aware of their backgrounds

Openness

and know identifying information. Ongoing relationships with significant non-biological caregivers or mentors may provide desired continuity with the child's history.

THEOLOGICAL CONSIDERATIONS

Reflecting on the issue of openness can lead Christian PAPs to consider biblical teaching about honesty. Proverbs establishes honesty and words of truth as an ethical standard (Prov 22:21; 24:26), yet the New Testament clarifies how truth and love go hand in hand (1 Cor 13:6; Eph 4:15; 1 John 3:18). Honesty is more than sharing cold, hard facts! John equates the second and third persons of the Trinity with truth (John 14:6, 17; 16:13; 1 John 5:6), and both speak truth (John 8:40, 45–46; Acts 28:25). That said, although God always speaks truthfully, he does not always speak fully. God reveals the plan of salvation, for instance, to Adam and Eve (Gen 3:16), yet details about Jesus' lineage or the nature of his sacrifice come to light only through progressive revelation at the appointed times.

The biblical concept of truth-telling offers Christian PAPs insights that can be applied to adoptions across the openness spectrum. Clearly, Christian PAPs should be people of their word. There is no place for signing an adoption agreement but failing to keep it. Adoptive parents further express love for their children by sharing with them as much as possible about their stories, but wisdom is necessary. For example, if the adoptee was conceived through prostitution or rape, or if a birth parent is deceased, parents should seek words that are true but age appropriate, and a pattern of progressive revelation may help children process the information. Before sharing that a birth parent is incarcerated, adoptive parents might help their child develop a concept of prison as a place where adults who make sad choices go for a long timeout instead of thinking of it as a place where bad people are locked up. Even when the truth is painful, knowledge brings freedom from unhealthy speculation.

Thinking about Adoption

When facts about the actual birth family are unknown, adoptive parents can suggest the most plausible scenarios and maximize what is known about the child's background. For instance, following a closed adoption from China, you might explain to your daughter how laws aimed at limiting population growth and family size prompt parents to relinquish children they would have otherwise raised. You can plan to foster positive connections by remembering significant caregivers from the orphanage, or by maintaining contact with others who have adopted from the same location.

Decisions about openness are deeply personal, but they shape the lives of adoptive parents, birth families, and adoptees in significant ways. Our children's adoptions are semi-open, each for a different reason. Pictures of our children's birth moms appear in their baby books, and their adoption stories are part of the ongoing narrative of our lives. Whether you envision ministering Christ's love to your child's birth mother through a healthy open relationship or whether you will protect your children with a closed arrangement, you can still pursue honesty, truth, and wisdom as you discuss your adopted children's origins and identities with them.

REFLECT AND RESPOND

Read about families with adoptions on the closed end of the spectrum in appendices 2, 4, 5, 7, and 8, and families with adoptions that are more open in appendices 1, 2, and 3.

- How much do you know about your own family of origin, their background, and history? How has this knowledge shaped your own identity? What difference do you think it would make if you did not know these things?

Openness

- Try to imagine the perspectives that each member of the adoption triad might have regarding various degrees of openness. What fears and concerns emerge? What opportunities and benefits? Record your reflections on the chart below.

	Closed	Semi-open	Open
Birth family			
Adoptive parents			

Thinking about Adoption

Adoptee			

- In light of what you have read in this chapter, if you pursue adoption, do you think you would prefer a closed, semi-open, or open arrangement? Why?

- Are there any arrangements that you would not consider? Why not?

Openness

- Having considered the various paths to adoption, the wide range of options, and theological reflections, do you discern a calling to become an adoptive parent? If so, what is your next step? If not, now that you know more about the needs and challenges that PAPs, waiting children, and adoptive families face, how might you minister to and encourage them?

Appendix 1

Melissa and Rob Levitt[1] are the parents of a two-and-a-half-year-old daughter, Kenzie, who joined their family in 2013 through a lawyer-facilitated private adoption.

Melissa: We have always had adoption as part of our families since both of us have siblings who were adopted. As I remained single in to my late thirties, I began to feel a call to adopt to the point that I even started saving money to use towards adoption. When we began dating, Rob knew that adoption was a possibility, particularly because we were both somewhat older. Once we were married, we both had a heart for adopting and immediately began the process to be certified.

We experienced nothing but support from family and friends. My mother was particularly excited because she had an adoption story of her own, and many in Rob's family rejoiced when they learned that the adoption would connect them more to their Cherokee heritage and background.

Rob: As we began exploring our adoption options, we discovered that we would be eligible under the Indian Child Welfare Act to adopt a child through a Native American tribal government because I am part Cherokee. We coordinated the adoption through the tribal Children's Services Department and a private lawyer who specializes in adoption.

---

1. All names have been changed to preserve the privacy of the families who have shared their stories.

Appendix 1

Both: It took nine months to complete our application, physicals, background checks, Cherokee heritage paperwork, training, and home study to become certified to adopt. It was not difficult, but there were a lot of forms and details. Within a month we were matched with a birth mother who had just delivered, and a week later, Kenzie was placed with us.

Inclusive of travel and incidentals, the adoption cost us about $30,000. To assist with the finances, we were able to take advantage of an adoption reimbursement that was available through our employer, and we got some funds back through the Adoption Tax Credit. Additionally, the years of savings along with a family gift that paid for our hotel helped to cover the costs.

This particular adoption involved three governing bodies: our home state, the state where Kenzie was born, and the Native American tribal government. All three had slightly different regulations, which complicated matters and slowed down parts of the process. For instance, the paperwork for the Interstate Compact on the Placement of Children (ICPC) that would allow Kenzie to cross state lines was slow, and there were some missteps. The lawyer did not realize that the tribal government required surrenders to be completed in front of a judge, so the surrender had to be done twice. Another worker dropped the ball on a piece of paper for about a week, and we didn't know to ask about it.

There was a lot about the process that we did not know until afterwards, so it ended up taking a month for the ICPC to clear. But our lawyer had a deal with an extended-stay hotel for families waiting for the ICPC clearance so we had a little rocking chair in the room, and we interacted with several other adoptive couples. It was both encouraging and frustrating, though, because normally their stays were about a week and a half, and ours was so much longer. However, we had a wonderful time bonding as just the three of us before getting home and having everyone come and see our new arrival.

Another tricky part of our process was that Kenzie's birth state said that adoptions were not revocable after surrender, but it did not allow adoptive parents to file for finalization until a year

Appendix 1

after placement. The Native American tribal government, on the other hand, mandated that adoptions be revocable until finalized. For us, this meant that it took eighteen months from placement to finalization, with the adoption being revocable the entire time. This was extraordinarily difficult, especially because we hadn't intended to enter into a high-risk placement. We were terrified at the risk of opening our hearts knowing what might happen. Particularly in those initial days, on top of adjusting to having a newborn, we were also worried about what the birth parents were thinking, what the lawyers were doing, and if we were ever going to get home. It was so much more complex than what biological parents experience, and it felt like we were flooded with emotion all the time.

Rob: At the outset I did wonder if it would be difficult to bond with a child who was not mine biologically, but when the time came, it was not an issue. Sometimes I am even surprised by how much those thoughts just do not come up. I have come to understand that relationships that are intentional and chosen can be incredibly deep. Kenzie is my child, and most of the time the word "adopted" doesn't need to be used as a modifier.

Melissa: As part of our bedtime ritual I sing a song to Kenzie that includes her story that she's adopted and that God sent her to our family. As a result she knows that she is adopted, although at her young age she does not have full understanding of what that means so we know we're planting seeds for the future. We do not ever want her to remember a time that she was told that she was adopted. We do not consider it to be a source of shame or anything negative, so we want her to know from the outset.

Both: We have maintained an open relationship with Kenzie's birth mother by talking on the phone and sending pictures several times a year. Initially we were fearful about the relationship, particularly before the adoption was finalized. On some level we would understand someone becoming emotionally undone after placing a child so we did not know how we would navigate that ongoing relationship. There were fears there, but over time we have become significantly less worried about that. Since having Kenzie we have realized that you cannot have enough people love you. It is a responsibility and an honor to be an adoptive parent, but we are just part of her life, and the birth family is still very much a part of her life even if they are not physically present. We intend to let Kenzie determine what sort of a relationships she will have with her birth mother and biological siblings as she gets older. At some point we do plan to take her places to learn more about her Cherokee heritage, and we want to expose her to things like the Cherokee alphabet and language when it's age appropriate.

Because Kenzie looks very similar to us, at times people have commented, "She looks like she could be yours." Although we know what they mean, we do not care if she looks like us or not. She is our daughter no matter what she looks like, so it can be frustrating to think that people think it is an issue. Depending on the circumstances, sometimes we respond by correcting and teaching people, and other times we smile, and nod, and let it go.

We have seen how our adoption experience has allowed us to make connections with other adoptive parents. There is a bond that forms quickly when you know that they have gone through a process that is very difficult and that you know about. Everyone's story is different, but you have some idea of how to relate to them and how to pray for them.

Melissa: One of the best parts of being an adoptive parent is simply being a mother that I have always wanted to be. It is even better than I could have imagined. I had a lot of years of being upset about not having children, so I grew in understanding that God has a plan and that he has it under his control. I need to trust that more, and that has been one of the best parts of the adoption process since it has grown my faith in Christ. I do not have to be as worried or anxious because God's got it all under control. God sent me Rob and then Kenzie at the right time and in the right way, and I could not have picked it any better.

Rob: Being adoptive parents has given us more insight into how God works in our lives, and it has been an avenue for him to teach us more about love, vulnerability, sacrifice, patience, and faith. The adoptive process has shown me that God is always

Appendix 1

working even when we do not know it. He took this little baby born in a different state and put her in our family intentionally. Even when we are not aware of it, he is always at work. In the huge things or the everyday things, he's at work fulfilling the plan that he has for each of us.

Melissa: If you are considering adoption, pray about it and make sure you have a clear path. I felt like I had prayed for years by the time we were ready to fill out paperwork. It might not be like that for everyone. Rob did not know it was the plan until we had Kenzie. But it is an important thing to pray about it and see what is put on your heart and to understand that it is a very hard process, but it is also more rewarding than anything you could ever do.

Rob: Also try not to allow the small things to rile you up. It is important to understand that it is not like putting a hammer to a nail. A lot of things have to happen. There is a lot of waiting. There is a lot of knowledge you have to have, and sometimes you do not know until after you should have had it. Do not let that frustrate you. Have confidence in the Lord's word to you and go forward. Have your eyes open, and be diligent and a good steward, but know that you will not have control. The ultimate outcome may not go the way you want it to go, but in God's sovereign nature you play a part in the lives of every child that is put in front of you, and you can trust in that. There is a reason you were involved even in failed placements. We may not always see it, but we trust that it is there. Be patient and wait on the Lord.

Appendix 2

Ted and Jen McDougall are the parents of two children, Joey (age four) and Michelle (twenty-two months), through interracial, private domestic adoption.

Jen: Adoption was something that Ted and I talked about even before we got married, and it was always part of the plan. We pursued biological children first but walked through several years of infertility. Then we attended an interest meeting at the agency we ended up using for our son's adoption, and we prayed about it for a long time. I was ready to start the adoption process a full year before Ted was.

Ted: I always felt sure that it was the right thing for us, but I had the story of Abraham in my mind. God tells him he is going to have a child, but Abraham takes matters in to his own hands, and he has a child the wrong way. I feared that we were supposed to wait, and I did not want to outrun what God had planned. After one particular weekend away, I became very confident that adopting was a holy desire. It was not the wrong way to do the right thing. It was time to move forward.

Initially, it seemed like there was just one question to answer: Do we adopt or not? But once we answered yes, we discovered there were endless decisions to make. Domestic or international? Special needs or not? Infant or older? Each decision seemed massive and overwhelming to me. We felt very at peace and called to adopt, but we encountered people with strong opinions about the

Appendix 2

different types of adoption. That played into my insecurities about not wanting to make the wrong choice. But we were reminded of the big picture that every child needs a home, and there are so many right ways to do it.

Jen: Because I grew up overseas, I had always envisioned international adoption. We initially applied for a South Korea program through a leading Christian agency, but discovered that it was not accepting people at that time. That is when we started to think about domestic.

Both: Ultimately we selected a small, local agency that only did open adoptions. We completed the piles of paperwork, fingerprinting, medical check-ups, our home study, and twelve hours of training that were required to be approved. Our agency's fee was based on income, and since we earned very little, we paid just $12,000, and they allowed us to make payments along the way.

Our agency was connected to a thriving ministry to birth mothers that worked with twenty different women at any given time. Some would choose adoption. We loved the care that these moms received, but for several months none of them chose adoption, which meant that we waited. Ultimately, we waited for two years, and it was hard. I wish I had been in a place where I could have trusted more fully that God would do what we thought he said he would do.

Our friends and family were overjoyed and supportive of our decision to adopt, but one family member asked what we would do if the child chose to go live with his/her birth family some day. There was some anxiety there because you see things in the news, but our agency was quick to assure us just how rare the horror stories are.

Three different times we were matched with birth mothers, but the adoption plan fell through at various stages during their pregnancies. Even though we had tried to remain guarded, we sobbed with heartbreak each time. Then one Friday we received *the* call. A birth mother had relinquished her week-old baby at a fire station under our state's Safe Haven laws. He came home to us on Monday, and the adoption was finalized seven months later. All we know of his history is that his birth mother is African-American. His paperwork says abandoned infant, and his little baby footprints say Baby Boy Doe.

This part of Joey's story has been surprisingly difficult. Joey has a lot of anxiety and a fear of abandonment that seems to go deeper than that of the normal four year old. We recognize that he only became ours because of brokenness and not because of something good. God brings beauty from ashes, and we hope Joey will come to see God's hand in his incredible story, but as his parents, it is hard to know he has pain that we cannot take away. We can only help him walk through it.

We adopted our daughter, Michelle, two years after Joey. By then we had moved to a different state and could not use our previous agency. As we were considering our options, an acquaintance approached us about a pregnant fifteen-year-old girl who wanted to make an adoption plan so we proceeded with a private adoption through lawyers. In hindsight we preferred working with an agency over a private lawyer because it felt like all of the parties were taken care of better when there was a case worker assigned to each one.

Michelle's adoption is completely open. We got to know and love her birth family, and we know they love Michelle. We were able to be there for Michelle's birth, and we have maintained regular contact through a private blog, texts, and phone calls. Long term we want Michelle to be able to have that relationship on her own terms, so while she is young we are trying to keep the options open for her.

Both of our children come from ethnic backgrounds that differ from our own. We were open to a child of any race, and part of our training prepared us to be a conspicuous family. Michelle's skin tone is quite light, and she is still too young to understand, so most of our experience so far relates to Joey. We are working to surround him with strong black men and to make sure that his world reflects not only diversity but families that look like ours. We have initiated conversations about race with him. We have put our arms next to each other, and we have had to tell him, "You don't look like you belong to us so we have to make sure we act and behave like we belong to each other." There are times we will ask if he understands what we are saying, and he says no, but we know we are planting seeds for when he is older.

Our families are from the South, and while they supported our interracial adoptions in theory, there are issues. They love our children, but they say inappropriate things about other black people or about racial issues in the news, so we cannot always be around them. One family member has made an incredible transformation. He told us that he was never bothered by racist things people said before, but that changed after Joey came home. He no longer hears the comments in the same way, and he wanted to punch someone for making a joke.

In grocery stores we have all sorts of insensitive interactions with strangers asking if Joey is ours, if he is adopted, where he is from, and more. We live in the thick of the South, and we have people who tell us that they just love our "ethnic babies." Or they will say weird things like that they are jealous of their hair or their skin. So we are learning to navigate when to ignore, when to educate, and when to confront.

Jen: I love having a family that reflects the world a little bit more than a homogeneous family does, but I am very sensitive to not wanting my kids to pick up a cause just because of what our family looks like. The other day someone asked me, "Aren't you glad God didn't give you biological children?" And I agreed because I cannot imagine anything else. But although we adopted, we were not drawn to adoption as a cause. It is just how God built our family. We are very committed to adoption, and we advocate for it, but I just love the kids.

Ted: It has been a special delight as an adoptive family to see our children develop traits and behaviors that look like us. Joey did something the other day that made my mom laugh and describe how I had done the same thing when I was little. Since we frequently hear how different our children are from us, that moment was really touching. That is when you feel that unique family bond,

Appendix 2

and I think you might take those things for granted on some level in a biological family because you expect similarities.

Now that I have adopted children I see more clearly the Bible's teaching that all Christians are adopted. All of us enter God's family in the same way, which is by God's choice. We are very careful and sensitive to never take on a savior mentality. We did not save our children by choosing them. I do not ever make that connection. But I feel a greater sense of confidence in God's love for me now. The biblical theme of God's pursuit, of choosing even when it is hard and he is not getting anything in return—that active love on God's part is something that I had just missed before, but now it is so clear.

Both: If you are considering adoption, then take a step forward. Go talk to someone. Sit down with a case worker. Apply and see what happens. Do not just sit, pray, and try to figure it out on your own. Go learn more about it and let God speak to you during the learning process. You get more clarity as you take a step. It can be hard to hear the voice of God if you are not putting yourself out there.

There are a lot of right steps in adoption and fewer wrong ones than you think. You just have to embrace the speed bumps along the way. Nothing is going to be smooth. Adoptions don't work that way. But nothing is going to be wasted if you embrace it.

Appendix 3

The Wallace family includes Bruce and Sandy and their children, Allie (age eleven), Kayleigh (age eight), Paul (age five) and Kristy (age four). A private domestic agency placed each child in the family during infancy.

Sandy: Early in our marriage, Bruce and I ran into infertility issues. After testing we chose not to seek treatment. My extended family includes a number of adoptees over several generations so the idea of adoption was not unusual for me. At work I had also run support groups for teen moms, so I had heard many personal stories from birth mothers, adoptive mothers, and adoptees.

Bruce: I did not have much experience with adoption, but we knew we wanted to be parents, and that outcome seemed most likely through adoption. I was a little worried, but an adoptive father I knew assured me that I would be able to love a child who was not mine biologically.

Sandy: Sometimes people think that if you are on the infertility train, there are different stations with adoption being the last stop. I disagree. Adoption was a volitionally different decision. We exited the infertility train and boarded another train altogether.

Bruce: My parents were surprised and somewhat uncomfortable with our decision since they lacked any point of reference for adoption, but Sandy's mom had a terrific reaction. She said that she could not have been any happier if we had told her that we were pregnant.

Appendix 3

Both: A few families at church were pursuing foster-to-adopt, so we became certified parents through our county. One of the first things our adoption assessor said to us was that you cannot come through the county to get a kid for cheap, which was a really painful comment to us. At one point we took in a toddler for respite care thinking adoption was possible, but we soon learned she would be placed with another family that was caring for her sister. Ultimately it was clear that we were really at cross purposes with the county. We appreciated their push to reunify families, but we wanted permanency, so after a year and a half, we reconsidered our approach.

Sandy: I asked some social workers I knew from the obstetrics department of a local hospital to recommend adoption agencies that they thought showed great respect for birth parents. We interviewed quite a few agencies in our state before selecting one they had praised. We wanted to have a clear conscience and rejoice in the adoption process while knowing that the birth parents were well treated.

Bruce: Our agency director took a whole afternoon to meet with us and answer our questions.

Both: It is not a faith-based agency, but at that time Bethany Christian Services was not in our state. Catholic Charities and Lutheran Social Services were only doing one or two placements a year, and an average wait of four to five years did not appeal to us.

The agency we selected was able to accept our home study from the county, but we had to do another twenty-four hours of education with them. In the classes they said their average wait was a year, but anything could happen. We got the call for our oldest, Allie, in just three weeks! Then, three hundred sixty-four days passed from the time our paperwork went in until our second daughter, Kayleigh, was born. Since we were matched before her birth, we were able to spend the seventy-two hours in the hospital with her at her birth parents' request.

Our agency's process was to identify prospective parents whose preferences were compatible with the birth parents' desires. They presented each birth parent with the five matching families

Appendix 3

who had been waiting the longest. If the birth parent(s) did not select one, the agency would present another five. Kayleigh's parents saw the first set, which included ours, but then they asked to see them all! They looked through every waiting family the agency had before choosing us.

Sandy: We had found it awkward to market ourselves in the adoptive parent profile. How do you express all that you are and your desires and hopes in that format? We used to say that if you Googled "desperate," adoptive parent profiles would come up! I remember reading others' profiles that said how they loved the outdoors or cooking, but it seemed like everyone had the same stuff. Later we learned that we stood out to Kayleigh's birthmother because our pet rabbit had the same name as her pet dog. Here I was expecting something like, "Their love of Jesus just came through" or something equally profound!

Both: For our third child we were back in line waiting with our same agency when the social worker called and explained an unusual situation. A birth mother who was working with a different agency in our state had not found an adoptive family that she was interested in within that agency, so she got on the computer, and for five months she went through all kinds of waiting families in the state and came up with a short list. She had a very supportive group of women from her church, and she was praying that she would not go in to labor until she had selected a family. They all went out for coffee on a Sunday night and had five profile books, including ours, and they unanimously picked us. Then she went home and delivered a baby boy overnight. Paul was born on Monday, we got the call on Tuesday, and we brought him home at seven days.

Sandy: When Paul turned one, we decided to be on our agency's backup list of families who didn't want to be actively considered but who might be open to children who were more difficult to place. On the morning I planned to tell the agency our decision, they called me first about a baby. After praying, we said no to that particular match, but it got us thinking more fully about the realities of having a fourth. Thus, two weeks later when they

Appendix 3

called again with the news that Allie's birth mother had delivered a second baby girl, we were ready to receive this sibling. We happened to be at a vacation spot that was somewhat close to where Kristy was born, so we picked her up before returning home. Our neighbors joke about how we left on vacation with three kids, and we came home with four, while they just bring T-shirts home from their trips!

Sometimes adoptive parents love the idea of a birth mother placing a second child, but I don't necessarily share that. I am grateful for both of my daughters, but I think there is a lot of grief for the birth mom who makes an adoption plan, and to see someone go through it twice is hard.

Bruce: All of our adoptions are semi-open. Each birth mother shared identifying information, but we gave only first names. The agency only required us to send pictures once a month for the first year. It seemed terrible to go from sending photos once a month to not sending them at all, so several times a year we send a stack of pictures and a letter. We like that our birth parents do not have to look at every child at the mall and wonder if it is their child. They know the children are happy and healthy. We did set up a separate email address to communicate with two of our birth moms. We're really comfortable having both connections and boundaries like this.

Both: The costs of our adoptions varied. We spent about $18,000 with Allie's. Kayleigh's was $21,000 due to a home study update. Paul's was closer to $14,000 because the second agency waived some fees since the birth mom located us herself. Kristy's only cost $10,000. Our home study was still active, and there was no activation fee because we were on the backup list.

Sandy: We had some savings, and in each case we were able to have a large amount refunded to us through the Adoption Tax Credit. God provided in other, more unexpected ways too. For instance, a family from another church was awarded an adoption grant, but when they did not need the money, the church asked to give it to us. In another instance someone gave us an envelope with $500 to use towards Kayleigh's adoption. We thought we already had the costs covered, but when we went to pay, we discovered two additional, unexpected charges totaling $500!

Bruce: Our children all know that they joined the family by adoption. We told them as early as we could and read books that were specific for adoption. We have always kept it an open conversation.

Sandy: All of the adoptions finalized at around six months, and we know all those dates and celebrate them in addition to birthdays. We have seen that especially with Allie, birthdays are a little conflicted. She cried hard when she turned six and said she missed her birth mother. And we see behavior change around the time of her birthday, so she is very sensitive along those lines.

I also remember one time when Kayleigh was around four. She had been in time out, and I went to get her and talk about the time-out thing. When I asked if she had any other questions, she surprised me. "Why did my birth parents give me to you?" she wondered. It was a total ambush. I said they were very young. "Too young to change my diapers?" she asked. I said something else. "They didn't have any toys for me?" she responded. I eventually told her how very careful they were to pick a family for her and how they wanted to see every profile book that the agency had. This assured her that they loved her, and she was totally satisfied.

Bruce: Amazingly there are times we have forgotten that they are adopted. Once when the doctor asked about our daughter's medical history, we answered based on our own without thinking.

Sandy: Another time I commented to Bruce how funny it was that our niece and nephew are quite small, but our kids are so much bigger! And Bruce just looked at me!

I did have one uncomfortable experience in the library not long after Kayleigh was born. A stranger overheard me talking with a friend about Kayleigh's adoption, and she started asking questions across the children's section of the library including how much she cost and other things that are on the classic "what you don't say" list. It threw me mostly because I knew Allie was listening. As a result I decided in the future to respond by saying "Oh, are you interested in adoption? Because I'm here to enjoy the

Appendix 3

library with my children, but I'd be happy to give you my phone number if you want to talk more."

Bruce: I love seeing how God put our family together in such a purposeful way. Once someone asked me if I ever miss having a biological child. I explained how I feel sad for people who don't get to experience adopting.

Sandy: The best part of being an adoptive parent is having a totally different perspective on the Lord's adoption of us, which is another thing that I did not see coming. We saw his hand in ways that were amazing and that we never could have scripted. I also love how the adoption community cares for one another and adopts one another in a way.

Of course, no one should feel pressure to adopt. These days in the church there can be a trendiness to it. A friend who has not adopted once said to me that you almost feel like you are not quite a good-enough Christian if you haven't adopted! Wow! But you can have a heart for orphans and follow James 1:27 without adopting. Not everyone is called to it. People need to pray and talk honestly with each other. They should make sure they are getting wise council about going ahead with their eyes wide open. For us, adoption was part of our calling.

Bruce: If you are praying about it and wondering if it is the right thing to do, it will be made clear. That does not mean that there won't be a point where you have to go for it, but never do it out of guilt. It should be a calling, and if it is, go for it. And if it is not your calling, that is okay. God has another way for you to serve.

Appendix 4

Blake and Helen Burrow are the parents of Eva (thirteen months), who joined their family as an infant through transracial, private domestic adoption.

Helen: We got married straight out of college with the thought that we would wait a few years before having kids, but it was actually eight years before I started feeling open to the idea. By then we knew a number of couples who had adopted, and we were strongly considering adoption rather than even trying biologically. We just did not have a strong desire for a biological child.

I began researching adoption. My first priority was to find professionals who knew what they were doing and who had a record of good customer service. I was not necessarily looking for a Christian agency, but I quickly came across the leading private Christian adoption agency in the United States, and it was evident that they were good at what they did.

Blake: We had been getting information from a lot of agencies that almost sounded like puppy mills. It was all a business transaction. The Christian one felt different to us in that regard, so we made our choice.

Helen: We were confirmed in our call to adopt through a series of things. We knew we had the ability to adopt. We were starting to feel passionate about it. And I felt at peace about doing it, which was significant because I had been terrified about the whole idea of having children. After attending an information

Appendix 4

session hosted by our agency, I was certain this was something that we should be investigating, and we started the process. We chose the agency's domestic program almost by default. We did not feel pulled toward international, and we felt like there were enough kids near us who needed families. Each step of the way we felt at peace even when we were outside of our comfort zone and questioning how long it would take, how much it would cost, and how we would respond if we were to have a failed placement.

Both: When we told friends and family our plans, everyone was supportive but curious about our decision and the process. One asked overtly whether we had even tried to get pregnant, thinking that adoption was only a Plan B for couples struggling with infertility. Another jokingly wondered whether we would go look through a one-way mirror and pick out a baby!

In reality our agency required us to attend an information session prior to submitting an application. After it was approved, we went as a couple for an initial screening interview that was a two-hour long review of questionnaires about our background. More detailed paperwork and individual interviews followed. We completed thirty-six hours of classes and wrote several book reports. Then we finished up our home study and put together a profile book about our family that could be shown to birth parents who might consider us. Once the home study was approved, we began the wait.

Helen: Early in the process we completed a preference sheet regarding what sort of child we were open to parenting. There were nearly fifty different things that we had to decide! It felt so unnatural and took a while for us to process. We kept most things open, like gender and race and such, and we indicated that we would at least consider everything.

The agency has each birth mother also complete a preference sheet, which the pregnancy counselor compares with those from prospective parents to find possible matches. If the birth mother wants to select the family for her child, she can view the profile books for any of the compatible families, and she can even choose to have a mediated meeting at the agency with up to three possible

Appendix 4

families. If for any reason the birth mother wants the agency to select a family for her, then they choose the compatible family that has been waiting the longest.

We moved through the whole approval process in just five months, which was rather quickly. I made a spreadsheet of everything to stay organized. Even though it was a lot of work, I really appreciated how our training focused on the birth parent experience, which gave us a lot of empathy for them. And the Christian aspect during the training allowed us to have conversations related to our faith. Figuring out the balance between making choices and trusting God was one of the biggest faith struggles for me, especially when it came to the preference sheet. On the one hand I wanted to be wise and responsible. As first-time parents I questioned our ability to handle something like a child with serious psychological issues, but I did not want to put God in a box, and I trusted that God would equip us to parent whatever child he had for us.

Blake: The agency had said that a placement could take anything from four months to five years so we did not know what to expect next. Three weeks in we got a call that we were being considered by a birth mother, but we soon learned she had selected another family. Honestly we were a bit relieved because it would have been almost too soon.

Our social worker wisely advised us not to plan our lives around waiting for a call, so apart from attending several support group sessions for waiting families, life returned to normal. It was so surreal because after those intense first months, we almost forgot we were in the adoption process for the next year and a half. The agency needed updated paperwork every year, and we had completed the one-year update, but as the second year approached, we were wondering whether we should do it.

Helen: Around that time our social worker called. I figured she wanted to remind us to start updating. Instead she was calling about the placement of a baby girl, who was three days old. We took the several days to think things over before we confirmed that

Appendix 4

we were ready, never imagining that another ten weeks would pass before Eva would come home.

Although the birth mother signed surrenders quickly after the birth, the agency had great difficulty locating the birth father. When they did, we learned that he had not known about the baby, so there was an ongoing saga while he decided whether to raise her. The agency deemed it high risk to let Eva come home with us in the interim, so she stayed with a foster mother employed by the adoption agency, and we were able to visit her for one hour each week. Ultimately the birth father signed the surrenders, but since our state allows birth parents a thirty-day revocation period, in order to bring her home we had to sign additional papers acknowledging that the placement was still at risk during those initial days.

In the six months after Eva came home, the social worker completed three post-placement visits to check that everything was going okay. That cleared us to start the finalization process, which meant hiring a lawyer and petitioning the court for adoption since those services weren't covered by our adoption agency. We got a court date just before her first birthday, and after going through such a lengthy adoption process, we were amused that we spent less than 60 seconds in the courtroom for the finalization!

Both: In total, the adoption cost nearly $40,000. Blake's work offered $3,500, and we had an inheritance that covered the rest. We do want to adopt again, though, which will require us to explore other funding options.

Helen: At this point Eva is still too young to understand her adoption. Nonetheless we want to set the stage now and intentionally talk about it in natural ways. For instance, I just told her, "You have beautiful eyes. I wonder what your birth mom's eyes are like." Or on her birthday we told her that we were thinking about her birth mom and how she must have been so brave and loved her so much. We want her to recognize that her birth parents were in difficult places, and we'll continue to have that discussion with her in age-appropriate ways.

Blake: The fact that Eva is African-American and we are not makes it pretty obvious that she entered the family by adoption.

Appendix 4

We were open to TRA from the outset, but it was one of the things we researched the most once we were in the process. We were shocked to read that some people think it is harmful for the black community and for the child. We did not want to harm a child, so we had to ponder that. In the end we determined that we were comfortable with it. Living in a very diverse urban context helps. But we had to think through family relationships.

Helen: My grandfather is overtly racist, so now that we have Eva, he is completely out of the picture partly by his choice and partly by ours.

I'm learning hair as I go, but I have several friends who are helping me. One colleague, who is a black woman, specifically told us, "I don't want that child walking around with white mama hair." So I'm sensitive to that issue, and I do not want to take Eva out in public and have people think poorly of me because her hair is not done well.

Our biggest plan is to avail ourselves of people and places in our area who can be resources. It is easy to set her up with people who are the same race as her or who represent many different races, who can help guide her and mentor her and come alongside of us. Eva has an honorary grandma who is an older African-American woman, and she is great. In our house, we are trying to be intentional about what artwork we display. We think carefully about the variety of books that we are reading with her. I am studying the psychology of racial identity and have learned some great things there.

We have frequently had people ask us where she is from, and when I say right here, there is this awkward pause. People seem so disappointed. They are expecting Ethiopia or such because there is this idea that black children come from "over there," and somehow it is more acceptable if they came from a foreign country. One random stranger, who was a white guy no less, went so far as to tell me he thought her ancestry must be a mix of Ethiopian and Malawi! What was that?

Both: Walking through the adoption process made me think more about the biblical doctrine of adoption. It is a real picture of

Appendix 4

Christ choosing us and pursuing us so unconditionally. Eva did nothing to enter into our family, but over and over we had to say yes to keep going. Having that tangible picture is encouraging to our faith.

Blake: I am bothered when people comment that adopting Eva was such a nice thing that we did. We think it is the right thing for us to do, but it was not a charity case. She is not a cause. She is not lucky to be in our family. I mean, hopefully she is. But we are blessed even more.

Helen: I bristle with that too. I do not know if it is for myself or for her. There is an element of pity for her in that mentality. Oh, you saved this *poor* child. I want her to be able to stand on her own and not just be seen as this poor soul that got saved by these parents.

I think that idea devalues birth parents too and assumes that they are horrible. Despite her birth parents' situation, we have a lot of respect for them for making what we think is a great choice. They were courageous and brave to make an adoption plan.

Blake: For other couples who are considering adoption, do not be scared about the paperwork and finances. Yes, it will cost a lot of money, and yes, it is intrusive, but think about the big picture of what you are trying to do rather than the stumbling blocks. Parenting of all kinds has hurdles to overcome. It is just different hurdles for adoption than for biological parenthood.

Helen: Do not be afraid to look into it. Go to an information session, do some research, or talk with people and have folks pray with you. It does not mean you are locked in. If you do move forward, find an agency or person that you're comfortable working with, and then trust them. And find that healthy balance about the process. Be aware, but do not freak out.

Appendix 5

Eric and Ruth Mason are the parents of Mara (age two), who joined their family at birth through interracial, private domestic adoption.

Both: Infertility issues were the primary reason that we turned to adoption, although even before infertility manifested itself we thought we might foster or adopt children some day. At one point during our infertility, we attended a workshop at our church about adoption. An agency came and shared loads of information, and several adoptive families shared their experiences, but it was another two years before we started the adoption process. At that time we researched different agencies and selected one that friends from church had used previously.

Eric: We never questioned that we would be parents, and since it was not happening naturally, by process of elimination it was going to be by adoption. Our friends and family reacted positively to our decision. My parents were excited since they were eager for their first grandchild.

Ruth: A few folks commented that we would probably get pregnant after we adopted.

Both: Since we had never been parents before, we were hoping to experience a child from birth. Private domestic adoption is really the only path that makes that possible, and we were able to afford it because we had been living with two incomes and no kids for a while.

Appendix 5

Eric: International adoption also just did not appeal to me. The travel would have used up all of my vacation time from work and left me unable to have any time to be home with the baby once we returned stateside. Plus I am just not very flexible when it comes to foreign environments.

Ruth: We applied and were accepted with our agency in February 2013. Once we put our minds to it, adopting was our top priority. The process was not hard, but it was work. We were required to complete three full-weekend training sessions. I was sick during one of the weekends, but we were not going to miss it and have to wait until the next cycle of classes, so I muddled through.

Both: After training they completed our home study, which required answering a ton of questions about each of us. By June the agency worker was nearly done writing the document when we had a small delay. She realized that we were on well water, which had to be tested. At first it did not pass, so we had to have someone shock the well and then get it retested. We remember thinking that "normal" parents don't have to go through this to have a baby!

Eric: During the home study we were presented with the sheet, that scary sheet, that asked us to indicate our preferences for a child. It was overwhelming. Our agency used the same form for all of their various kinds of adoptions, so some of it did not apply for infants. Obviously we did not expect our newborn to walk or speak English! We did not specify gender or race. Overall we just wanted the same possibilities that people have with a normal pregnancy.

Ruth: But we were not intentionally seeking a child who was going to have long-term special needs, although if it turned out that way, that would be okay. We opted out of infants who had alcohol exposure since that can have long-term consequences, but we were willing to take a child with drug exposure since the baby could go through withdrawal and recover.

Both: Once our name went on the waiting list, we did not know what to expect, but our wait was only about five months.

Ruth: I know some people have matches in place for seven or even eight months before birth, but not us. We got a phone call

Appendix 5

saying that a baby girl had already been born, and they wanted us to come to the hospital immediately.

Eric: Mara's adoption is a closed adoption, so we do not have all of the details. What we have pieced together is that the birth mother was not sure who Mara's father was. She was planning to raise the baby if her current partner was the dad. But when she saw Mara was interracial, she knew he was not the father, and she implemented an adoption plan instead.

It was only after delivery that she told the hospital she wanted to place the child. They contacted our agency, who took it from there. That is why it was a last-minute call and probably why the birth mother does not want further contact.

Ruth: Mara was born addicted to heroin, so she spent nearly four weeks in the hospital at birth.

Eric: We were with her at the hospital around the clock, and we had a whole guest wing that we were able to stay in at no cost. It was uncomfortable and noisy, but it was good to be able to be there to comfort and soothe her while she was weaned off drugs.

Both: Mara's adoption was finalized when she was about ten months old. We celebrated with a big party, but since then we have not really done anything to commemorate her adoption specifically. We made a picture book of her story, and we read it with her. She will look through it sometimes but then lose interest. We do not hide the fact that she is adopted from her, but she is too young to understand, and right now she just does not care. She is only two.

At some point if we adopt again and that adoption is open, I am sure that will bring up awkward situations and questions. Our training had brought up the benefits of open adoption both for birth families and for the adoptee, but since birth mom did not want it, there was nothing we could do.

We do make an effort to be sure that Mara sees people of different races, particularly African-Americans. But since her birth mother was Caucasian we do not feel that she is getting a terribly different experience racially with us than she would have had there since her birth father was out of picture. We have lots of friends

Appendix 5

who have adopted, so we do spend time with other families who look more like ours. And to some extent we try to we have relationships with people of other races at church, but it is hard to do intentionally without feeling like we are going up to someone and saying, "Hey, you're black. Can we be your friends?" That is awkward.

Ruth: Mostly we live our lives, and I do not think about it. A few times when we have been in public people have asked if she is my daughter. Sometimes my answer causes people to backpedal and say things that are hilarious, like that she looks just like me.

Both: Overall we had a pretty ideal experience adopting Mara. It took just nine months from our application until her placement, which was a pleasant surprise. Our second attempt at adoption was a different story.

Our in-state agency matched us with a birth mother through a second out-of-state agency. She had about three months to go in the pregnancy, and they explained that a prior match had fallen through. After a few weeks they discovered that the birth mom was trying to work through multiple agencies all at the same time in order to get money from all of them. Nonetheless, when the agency assured us that she had decided to work exclusively with them, we continued with the process since we were already in deep both emotionally and financially.

Eric: But when the birth mother's due date approached, we were told not to come because she was having second thoughts. We heard nothing for several weeks until we got news that she had delivered and already taken the baby home from the hospital. Ultimately we are not sure what all had transpired with her situation, but beyond that we discovered that the out-of-state agency was bankrupt. In fact, we eventually learned that they were on a list of agencies that had applied for but been denied Hague accreditation.

Ruth: It was a shock. We had really researched our in-state agency, but we did not do due diligence with the second one. I guess we thought that since we trusted our agency, we could trust any others that they chose to work with. In retrospect we should

Appendix 5

have done our own research. The whole thing was a big, expensive learning experience.

Both: Our cost for Mara's adoption was about $15,000. The failed adoption was more than $30,000 since the second agency had more expensive fees, and the birth mother costs kept increasing.

Eric: We were able to cover expenses with our savings, and the Adoption Tax Credit has allowed some of those funds to come back to us. Our state has an adoption tax credit that goes up to around $10,000, and the federal one goes a little higher than that. We discovered that somehow the state and the federal credits are distinct from each other, so it is possible that we will actually make a little money on our first adoption over a five year period through the tax credit. I do not feel that guilty about that considering that the Adoption Tax Credit is not available for the failed adoption, so that money is gone.

Both: We have found that the adoption process has forced us to trust God and pray a lot. We had to rely on him for strength when we were waiting to adopt and when we were in the hospital with Mara. We had to trust him when we went through the failed adoption, and we cling to his sovereign plan and draw on his strength as we look to the future.

Appendix 6

Carlos and Marcy Garcia's biological children, John (age twenty-six) and Rachel (age nineteen), were nearly grown when the family adopted Susan (age four) from Ethiopia in 2012.

Carlos: I was thinking we should try for a third child, and Marcy started talking about adoption.

Marcy: I had had a difficult second pregnancy. Plus I was becoming more aware of orphans in the world, so why not adopt? I did not see God telling us no.

Carlos: I was unsure until I heard a conference speaker talk about adoption from a spiritual perspective. At that point all kinds of signs related to adoption started popping up in our lives. They turned my heart, and I knew we should add to our family by adoption.

Both: Because we had older children, people were surprised to learn that we were looking to adopt a girl under the age of two. They thought we were crazy to start all over again, but our close friends encouraged us and even wrote letters of recommendation for us.

Marcy: We were attracted to intercountry adoption because we felt like the need of an orphan overseas was probably greater than that of a child in the United States, and we wanted to avoid the risk of having a failed placement. We did read books that scared us a bit about international adoption. Our biggest concern was whether our child would have physical or emotional problems

Appendix 6

or learning disabilities. I really just wanted to be a mom, not a nurse or a therapist.

Carlos: We also knew we would have to travel internationally to an unfamiliar country. We worried how people might respond to foreigners coming into the country for adoption.

Marcy: Race was a factor too, because our marriage is interracial (African-American and Puerto Rican). Our older kids suggested that we adopt from China, but we preferred a child that looked like she belonged to us. To look at Susan most people would not know that adoption is part of her story.

Carlos: We were considering Guatemala when we learned that it had closed to intercountry adoptions, so we turned to Ethiopia, and we experienced a lot of "God things" that confirmed that choice.

Marcy: For instance, at the grocery store one day I approached a stranger who was dressed in a way that made me wonder if she was Ethiopian. I explained our interest, not knowing how she might react. But she was moved to tears that we wanted to adopt from her country, and she invited us to go out to dinner at an Ethiopian restaurant with her family. We have become quite close with them, and they love our daughter so much. Culturally they are a tremendous resource.

Carlos: We searched online for Christian adoption agencies, and chose one with a good record and a commitment to broader ministries in the countries where they worked. The anticipated expense and wait were significant, but since adoption was our calling, those things couldn't stand in our way.

We submitted our application, selected the Ethiopia program, and completed the required training online. Everything went smoothly and quickly at first. Then we waited almost two and a half years for a referral, and during those years, Ethiopia started requiring adoptive parents to make two trips rather than just one.

Marcy: We finally got the call about Susan, and three months later made our first trip when she was seven months old. We had already decided that her pet name would be "Honey Bee," and when we met her at the orphanage she was wearing a shirt with

Appendix 6

a bee on it that said "Bee Happy." It felt like a sweet confirmation from God that she was our daughter.

Both: We stayed a week, but we had to leave and come back and wait for the visa. Our final clearance was held up when there was some difficulty locating Susan's birth mother since she was moving locations to find work, so we had just two days' notice to buy tickets for the second trip, which was a big expense. Susan was ten months old when we returned for our second week, went to court, and completed the adoption.

Carlos: In the end, the adoption took almost three years and cost over $40,000, both about double what we had expected! We did hold a fundraiser that allowed friends to contribute towards our second trip. Pride made us reluctant, and we feared people would judge us for choosing to adopt when we couldn't afford it. However, we were so moved by neighbors, family, and friends who wrote some pretty big checks. They said they were happy to be part of the process and to bless us in that way. My company also provided a $10,000 adoption reimbursement, and we have gotten some money back through the Adoption Tax Credit.

Marcy: Although we do not have any sort of continued contact with Susan's family of origin, we do have more information than most people who adopt internationally. Through our adoption agency, we hired a company to create a video of our experience. We ended up with two DVDs that are good records of both of our trips, but the third disc blew us away. They actually found Susan's mom in her village and recorded her talking to Susan, telling why she placed her for adoption and why she named her what she did. To see the little dirt hut where our daughter was born is amazing and very emotional.

Carlos: Susan understands that she is adopted and that she was not in mommy's tummy. We talk about her birth mother, and we pray for her every night. We read books to Susan that incorporate adoption, and we try to be as open as possible. She has watched our trip videos and she has seen all the pictures from our time in Ethiopia. She is very much aware of where she is from, but we are waiting until she is a bit older to show her the third DVD.

Appendix 6

Both: We celebrate her adoption with cupcakes on Gotcha Day. Every year on her birthday we replicate a photo we took the first time we met her where she is in between us and we are both kissing her on her cheeks. And we release balloons for her birth mom on Mother's Day.

Marcy: We regularly go to the Ethiopian restaurant to celebrate her heritage. Once we took part in a parade where we wore Ethiopian clothes and marched with a lot of other Ethiopian families. We went to a cultural camp last summer for families who have adopted from Ethiopia, and we plan to continue doing that. It was a unique experience for us because we were the only mixed-race couple in the midst of white parents with black kids.

Both: We love that we have new friends and special people in our lives now because of adoption, but there are hard moments, too, as we parent her. When there are issues we question whether we are making mistakes as parents or whether there are just things in her DNA that are coming out. And there can be a real emotional and spiritual battle. On days when we are frustrated, we can doubt whether we did the right thing. But then we repent because we know the Lord called us to this. We believe that God is for adoption. And we have to believe that he will sustain us through the parenting and the hard days.

Carlos: Anyone who is considering adoption should seek counsel from trusted friends and pastors and study what Scripture says about adoption. And pray, pray, and pray for wisdom so you don't just make emotional decisions or think that you are rescuing a child. Also do not go into it thinking that your son or daughter will be thankful that you adopted them. You will be disappointed! There might be that one compliant, thankful child, but it probably will not be yours!

Marcy: Both partners also need to be on the same page. You are both adopting. I know of one situation where the husband wanted to adopt but the wife did not. She was starting to think of just giving in, but I cautioned her not to unless her heart had truly changed.

Appendix 6

Both: We love seeing how God continues to work through us to encourage others to consider adoption. We shared our experience with one couple, and now they have an infant girl. It is special to see them with her and to know that our story was part of making that a reality.

Carlos: I have found that our decision to adopt has become an avenue to share the gospel with my coworkers because I cannot talk about adoption without telling the story of how God worked in my heart.

Appendix 7

Bill and Lydia Bailey started their family with two biological sons, Jimmy (age thirteen) and Carson (age ten). Daughters Naomi (age nine) and Joy (age three), who both have medical special needs, joined the family through intercountry adoption from China.

Lydia: My first sense of a call toward adoption came as a teenager when I watched a TV program about orphans in Ukraine. I was struck by a scene which showed any children who had an apparent flaw being sent to a handicapped institution with deplorable conditions. In that moment I did not know what I was going to do with the rest of my life, but I knew I was going to do something about that. It spurred me on in my professional calling to become a physical therapist, and in my personal calling I knew that I would be involved with adopting a child from another country. Later when I was dating Bill, I let him know that if he was with me, adoption was part of my calling.

Bill: I had no real background with adoption and until that conversation with Lydia, I did not have it as part of my plan. But I liked her so much that it sounded fine to me.

Lydia: Over the years our interest turned toward a daughter from China. We had seen several China adoptions by people around us, and at that point China was at the forefront of international adoptions. It became more real to me the day I found out I was pregnant with my second boy. I think some part of me

Appendix 7

wondered if the adoption call would come to fruition if I had been pregnant with a girl, so being pregnant with my second boy served as more confirmation of God's call.

Both: We researched several agencies before submitting an application to a Christ-centered agency in July 2007. Our church family and friends were all supportive when we shared the news. Family had a harder time understanding, asking why we would want to do this to our family, especially when we already had two beautiful boys.

We went in wanting to adopt a healthy child. We remember thinking that it is sweet that people adopt special needs kids, but that is not our family. But after a conversation in which an agency worker explained that the wait for healthy children was significantly longer, we felt burdened. We questioned why we would get in a long line of people waiting for a healthy child if our heart for adoption was to minister and meet a need. Why were we doing this at all if we were trying to keep it safe? So we got the special needs application.

Lydia: Initially the list of diagnoses we would consider included only things that can be repaired or conditions that would not affect the child long-term. Because I am a physical therapist, we were open to children with orthopedic conditions. In August 2008, our first referral came in for a little girl with arthrogryposis, which meant she was missing certain muscles, some bones did not develop, and she had deformities. We showed her chart to a friend who is an orthopedic surgeon, and he scared us when he explained that she may never sit upright, and we could spend the rest of our lives caring for a child who is bedridden, so we said no. But God ended up using that to open our minds to what was coming. We started researching and considering conditions that were a little more involved so that when we got another referral in January 2009 for a two-year-old with the same condition, we were ready to say yes. We still had concerns, particularly regarding the long-term costs that we might face to take care of all of her needs, but this time we were able to have faith that God would take care of it because we knew he had called us to her.

Appendix 7

Bill: I was a little anxious about whether I would be able to love a daughter. I grew up with brothers, so I have only loved two women in my life: my mom and my wife. But while we waited for clearance to travel to get Naomi, we were able to send a care package to her. We sent her a pillow we had decorated with a screen print of our faces, and one day we received a picture back of Naomi in China holding our pillow, and it was incredible. It was like divine heart surgery. God cleared the way and made room in my heart for this little girl. I knew she was mine, and I was ready.

Both: The most stressful part of the process was waiting for our travel clearance. We were told we could travel as early as March, and we regularly checked a website that created timelines based upon when people were getting referrals, when things got processed, and when they traveled. Looking back, it was not a good idea to compare our process and timeline with others. We saw lots of people getting their approvals, but we were not, and we did not know why.

Our agency sent one team each month, and each month they said we would probably make the next trip. We were hopeful in May, but then swine flu hit and nobody was traveling because of it, so we had more delays. In June we learned that our approval would have to be in by Friday, July 3 for us to make the July travel group. We prayed for what we called "a July 4th miracle," but when we called the office to check, it was closed for the holiday. On Monday we learned that our clearance had indeed arrived on Friday, but we missed the window to travel because it had not been processed on Friday. Well, the mama bear in me came out, and the worker said she would see what she could do. Amazingly, we got the thumbs up on Tuesday, and we flew out on Thursday. Most people get nearly two weeks' notice, but we were not waiting any longer.

Lydia: After spending a few days in Beijing, we traveled to Naomi's province and orphanage. When we picked her up, she was terrified and crying. For the first several days she only wanted Bill, and she did not want anything to do with women. After five days in her province we traveled to the Embassy where she had to have

Appendix 7

a medical visit, and she needed to be sworn in as an American citizen to get her passport so she could leave the country.

Bill: It took us two years from the time we applied until we had Naomi home, and the total cost was around $25,000. But because the process had taken so long, Lydia had been able to work extra, and we had been able to save, so we were financially prepared for it.

Naomi is nine now. She knows she is adopted, and we make a bigger deal out of Gotcha Day than we do her birthday. All we know about her background is that she was dropped in front of a hospital when she was a week old. She traveled back to China with us last year (when we went to get Joy), and she seemed to have a good time, but she was definitely American. When people would try to talk to her in Mandarin she looked at them like they were crazy. But we do have a close family friend who is from China, and she invests in Naomi and loves on her in ways that we think provide a helpful connection to her heritage.

Lydia: After Naomi, we thought we were done, but we ended up becoming foster parents for a while. Then I had the opportunity to go on a mission trip to China and work in the orphanages, and God opened the door in a completely unexpected way for us to adopt Joy, a little girl with a severe heart defect.

Bill: Expanding our family through adoption has been a gift in and of itself. We have powerful stories of God's faithfulness. We better understand the gospel and being adopted into God's family. I read the parts in the Pauline letters about adoption as sons and the spirit of adoption from a completely different context now. Previously my understanding of the cross was heavily oriented toward justification and the legal implications, but this has made it a lot more relational. I find theological significance in reflecting on the moment when she was not ours, then a judge banged a gavel, and she was ours, and now it is a process of bringing her into our family.

Lydia: The bonding process has been more challenging with the two who came via adoption. I had to work to go from being

Appendix 7

viewed as a caregiver to being accepted as a mother, so the hugs and "I love yous" that we have now are extra sweet.

Both: We would recommend three things for couples who are considering adoption. First, find an agency that you are comfortable with and that you really trust, and stick with them. Second, consider your motives and make sure you have moved from a simple longing to be a parent to a commitment to parent whatever child God has for you. Finally, we found it to be helpful to be open about our adoption process. We were blessed by support and encouragement from our friends and our church, and it will be amazing one day to find out all the ways people have been influenced by our testimony to God's faithfulness.

Appendix 8

Valerie and Richard Brodwell have adopted five children, all of whom are now adults. Gwen joined the family through independent infant adoption. Twins, Brooke and Brenna, arrived via a private domestic agency adoption. Avani and Jayesh (Jay) came from India as preteens.

Richard: We wanted to have children, but God put us in a situation where we were not able to have birth children. Those simple, ordinary means confirmed the call to adopt for me.

Valerie: By our third year of marriage we were earnestly looking to adopt.

Both: Independent adoption was attractive because our finances were limited. There was no Facebook then, so we sent letters to friends explaining our desire to adopt and our search for a possible birth mother. We connected very quickly with a pregnant woman who was already overdue. She agreed to a closed adoption, and delivered within the week. The lawyer did his part, and when Gwen was two days old, he carried her out the front door of the hospital and handed her to us. The total expense was only $2,000!

Valerie: We started the adoption process again when Gwen was a year old. Although we believe that God orchestrated the details of Gwen's adoption, we felt sad that her birth mom did not have counseling and other services, so we worked through a national agency this time. The long wait to be matched made us wonder whether God was leading us to consider an older child instead.

Appendix 8

When we phoned the agency to talk about that possibility, they shared that a birth mother had just selected us to adopt the twin girls she had recently delivered! Although the details were fuzzy, they disclosed that the birth mom had some sort of special needs, which meant the girls had an increased chance of something too. We trusted that God had sovereignly placed these children in our path, and it wasn't up to us to decide that the risk was too great. As things unfolded, Brooke and Brenna were diagnosed with Rett Syndrome during their preschool years.

Both: Around the time Gwen was starting school, and before we knew the extent of Brooke and Brenna's challenges, we felt called to grow our family again. It was such a great privilege to have adopted three infants already, so we wanted to step out where some other people might not and adopt an older child internationally. We had three countries to choose from, and we picked India because it was the only one that did not require adoptive parents to travel.

In those days, profiles of children were on the Internet, and we became interested in a particular child. When our agency confirmed that she was available, the orphanage revealed that she had a brother and asked whether we would be willing to adopt him as well! We agreed to move forward with both adoptions.

It ended up being sixteen months before they came home. The judge questioned our intentions in adopting two older children. He feared that we wanted babysitters or household servants, so he said that if we wanted to adopt them both, we would have to come to his court to explain our intent.

Valerie: It was already a year after we had started the process, and we had had contact with the siblings via letters, so we packed our bags. Traveling certainly added to the time and expense, but it meant that we got to visit the orphanage where Jay and Avani had lived since they were abandoned as infants.

Richard: It was not a place I would have wanted to grow up, but it was better than living on the street or in the slums. They were safe for the most part. They ate.

Appendix 8

Valerie: We do not know much of their stories, but they were left in a safe place, which ensured that they received care. To this day our knowledge of their orphanage years is also sketchy. They will relay conflicting information at different times.

They do not have baby or childhood pictures. They really grieved about those missing pieces especially when assignments came up in school and everyone else had videos and photos. But we saw God's hand in the fact that they had each other and were not alone in their experiences. For our part we tried to instill in them a sense of family. Even though they were someplace else for much of their first decade, God has always ordained that they would be part of our family.

Both: Avani and Jay were eight and ten when they came home. Gwen was six, and the twins were four. There were lots of transitions going on with culture and language. They lost their native language after four months, but they still could not speak English well, so that was tough! From the beginning we made a point of preparing Indian food and incorporating whatever culture we could for them without embracing Hindu religious practices.

Richard: We had about a six-month honeymoon period with Jay before things got very difficult. Almost overnight the apparent happiness was gone for him, and we reached out for help. We had guardianship of him and of Avani, but their adoptions had not been finalized so there was definitely talk about whether it was right for him and for us to go ahead with the adoption. We did, hoping that the security of finalization would help him. It did not, and eventually he was diagnosed with Reactive Attachment Disorder.

Valerie: We have been open with all the children from the beginning about them being adopted. From the beginning we used the words and we read books with adoption themes, but we carefully avoided language that said they were special because they were adopted. Even though we had closed adoptions and knew only the first names of their birth mothers, we made sure to speak of them with love and respect. The twins have never had interest in their birth mom and seem to be at peace with it. But Gwen had

Appendix 8

interest, angst, and lots of questions about why. She was conflicted, always, and thought about searching for her birth mom when she turned eighteen. We didn't discourage her at the time, and more recently we have offered to help if she feels strongly about it, but she hasn't pursued that with us.

Both: We loved each of our children the moment we saw them. We did not give much thought to long-term things or what their adult lives might be like. It was just where we were and what God had for us. Yet, as the years passed, all five of our children have been diagnosed with conditions that are lifelong.

Richard: This was God's plan for us in his sovereignty for sure, but I have no doubt that had we truly known about the challenges that Gwen and the twins had, we never would have adopted again. We have wondered why God let us go forward.

Valerie: We did not know the depth of what we'd be facing with Jay and Avani. The combination of the five of them was really difficult, yet is dealing with Jay's RAD any different from someone who has a biological child with mental illnesses? Is it specific to adoption? In some sense, yes, because it is attachment disorder, but Gwen has ADHD and epilepsy, which are not adoption-related things per se.

Both: Anyone who is thinking about adoption should prepare for the possibility of special needs. Will they come? Not necessarily. But do you need to prepare? Absolutely. We've experienced it, and we know enough other adoptive families to say, yes, you need to prepare yourself for that. You owe it to yourself to consider if you can handle the long-term implications of some sort of special need. We are at a point when their needs are influencing decisions about our careers since we know that there is an extra onus on us to be more prepared financially in the years to come to be able to care for them long term. What do Brooke and Brenna at fifty-five look like? Gwen?

Richard: We recognize just how much this whole path with infertility and adoption has changed our life. We will always be dealing with the challenges, and that is hard. We are not like other families. We have had heartache and days when we felt like we did not even know how to get to the next day.

Valerie: I guess we are getting to the point because of our ages and our kids' ages where we can look back. It is an interesting mix of kids that God has chosen to give us as our five, but what can we say? It is the crucible of life, but it has been God calling us to live this out and to weather this together. At times it has been really, really hard. We have grieved a lot in different stages, but we have learned to have a lot of compassion for other people. And we have peace that this is what God has purposed for us. We have been blessed to see God work through the trials, and we hope that God has used us as others within the larger Christian community and in our churches have watched our weak and imperfect family.

Richard: God chooses to humble us through our children. It is God's severe mercy. God is far more concerned with our holiness than he is with our happiness. Those have been valuable lessons for us over the years.

Appendix 9

Meet the Rogers family. Josh and Dina adopted their first child, Katie (age six) through the State. They added natural children, Rachel (age six) and Joel (age three), and they are currently in the foster-to-adopt process with Peter (nine months).

Dina: I always wanted to adopt, and during our premarital counseling Josh and I talked about the possibility of adopting. I was comfortable with the idea because the man who is my dad in every meaningful way is not my biological father. And I love the biblical example. There is not a clearer picture of what Christ has done for the church.

Josh: We were so young when we got married that we intended to wait several years to have kids, but the first year we were married we thought we had a surprise pregnancy. It put the idea of parenting in our minds sooner. We started talking about different options, and Dina suggested that we adopt our first child.

Dina: I thought it would demonstrate to her that she was not a backup plan in any way.

Josh: I felt that since we were emotionally, financially, and relationally stable enough to adopt, then we should do it, but I had no idea what to expect. When we told my mom our decision, she said that she would never to be able to love an adopted child as much as a birth child. That hurt. Now she regrets ever having thought that, and she almost favors our adopted daughter.

Appendix 9

Dina: My family was a lot more open to adoption, but adoption is only one part of it. What sort of child you adopt is a different element. I was very nervous to tell them that it could be an interracial placement.

Both: We were attracted to international adoptions, but that route was too expensive for us. We considered private agencies, but the cost was about the same. Some friends explained how they had adopted their children through the county, so we called the hotline that spring, and they made it all sound very promising and enticing.

Dina: Now we did not know that this was a foster-to-adopt thing. We thought it was just adoption. Josh embraced the difference right away when he started seeing the need, but I was concerned because the county emphasized reunification of children with their biological parents. I feared going through a disrupted placement, but I figured that we would accept only highly adoptable placements in order to minimize the risk.

Both: We took our time completing our thirty hours of training and other paperwork so we were not licensed until more than a year later. It took another six months before they contacted us about Katie, who was eleven months old.

Josh: Katie had been placed with a Christian foster family from birth. Even though she spent ten weeks in the NICU, the foster mom went in and held her every day. We still have a relationship with her, and she comes to birthday parties and other events.

Both: Katie's adoption is interracial because she is black, and we are white. It is also special needs since she had prenatal cocaine and alcohol exposure and was born at twenty-eight weeks. As a result, she has a sensory processing disorder and developmental delays. She has been tested for a lot of other things and has been in every kind of therapy. Because of her special needs classification, we receive a higher adoption subsidy for her, we were eligible for the Adoption Tax Credit even though we were not charged any fees for her adoption, and she is covered by insurance.

Dina: At the outset I was really concerned about Reactive Attachment Disorder, so we wanted a younger child. I felt that I

Appendix 9

could handle tough behaviors and other difficulties, but it would be heartbreaking to have a child who couldn't bond with us. Since we got Katie at eleven months, and she had been with a solid family from birth, I was surprised by some of her challenges. I had no idea how influential the prenatal time and the drug usage would be.

Josh: God's irony and huge answer to prayer is that Katie is overly attached. We have had to work on getting her to separate!

Dina: People have asked if we struggle with anger toward her birth mom, but we really do not. Even though it is a closed adoption, which is all we were willing to consider at the time, we learned that the birth mother herself had experienced unbelievable amounts of neglect and abuse and that she was a prostitute and homeless when she had Katie. What we know of her story makes us feel compassion for her.

Both: Katie's adoption finalized nine months after her placement. We went on to have two biological children, but we knew we wanted to have at least one more child. Since we had kept our license, we went back on the county's waiting list. We were so discouraged because over a year passed without a call of any kind, so we switched to a private Christian adoption agency. We were with them for another year and had only one possible match with a birth mom who ended up placing through another agency that offered her more incentives.

Dina: Ultimately we came back to the county. We had to redo all thirty hours of training and start everything again, but I liked how they had improved their curriculum to talk a lot about birth parents and birth parent relationships and to be more upfront about trauma-informed care-giving.

Both: We were relicensed this past year, and we considerably expanded our criteria this time.

Josh: By this point I do not think I would have said no to any placement.

Dina: Even for me it was tough to fill out that criteria sheet and think that we might be saying no to someone. Everyone needs a home, but our home cannot fit them all! Realistically we chose to keep Katie the oldest and preserve the birth order there, but we would take any child age four or under, and we indicated that we could take a placement of one or two children. Because we already have several children, we are more open to a situation where the outcome is uncertain.

Both: It was not long before we got Peter. We have had him just a few weeks, and his situation is very tentative. The goal is reunification with his birth mother within a year if she follows her case plan. We would love to keep him permanently, but we recognize that we can have a positive influence on his life even if it is only temporary.

Josh: The emotions are so complicated because we are bonded with Peter, but he might go back. I want him to be with us forever, but that means a failure on the part of his mom, which would not be good for her, so I am not rooting for that. I recognize that beauty for us would be grief for her.

Both: We love that God has called our family to adoption. We are very open about it with Katie and all the kids, and we have had some memorable situations as a result of being an adoptive family, particularly an interracial family.

Dina: Sometimes adults will ask Rachel if she brought a friend to whatever activity we are doing. And she just looks at them like they are so strange not to know that Katie is her sister.

Josh: Once Katie had a meltdown when we had to wait at the bus terminal in downtown NYC. Because of her special needs, her meltdowns are intense. She kicks and flails at me, and the goal is just to keep her from hurting herself. So I am walking around with her and she is screaming, "You took me from my mom. When am I going to see my mom?" That did not look good, and someone called the police to come check things out.

Both: Because the girls are so close in age, they like to say that they are twins, and I do not think they have any concept that they could not be twins. Sometimes Rachel beads her hair just like Katie. There is no concept that they are different. But not long ago Katie was on one side of the table and somehow the rest of us were on the other, and she observed that we all have light skin and she

Appendix 9

has dark skin. I started to tear up immediately, because up to this point she truly had not noticed it as significant.

Dina: We have prayed that Katie would never feel unloved or left out, especially once we started having natural children. We have a little saying that I start and Katie finishes. I say "Daddy and Mom," and she says "chose me." And I continue, "And you'll be Mommy's baby," and she says "forever." Then we both say, "You're adopted." It is precious.

Both: Perhaps we have gone overboard and made adoption sound too special because Rachel has cried before because she is *not* adopted!

Josh: Katie likes to see the life book we made for her. She will come to us and ask to hear her story. We love that wording because it is a whole story. It is not just how she was born or how she was adopted. Those things are just parts of her bigger story.

Dina: Even on the absolutely hardest days with Katie, I have never wished that we had not done this. When you birth a child, it is expected that you have that love, but when you have to choose to love the person, it is different. And I think that is how God loves us. He is not regretting his sacrifice for us, even on our worst days.

Appendix 10

Despite struggling through infertility and multiple miscarriages, Jon and Annie Baker birthed a son, David (age six), and then adopted a sibling group of Marissa (age five) and Nate (age four) via the foster-to-adopt process.

Jon: At the outset we considered private adoption, but the price tag was too high.

Annie: The Lord had been working in my heart for a few years about foster care. Multiple prior generations in my family had even been foster parents. But I thought I was not strong enough to handle the anguish and heartache of loving children and then having to let them go especially after having had miscarriages. Yet we kept coming across people who mentioned one particular Christ-centered child-placement agency with a foster-to-adopt program.

Jon: We called and eventually attended a training session. Looking back we might have been wiser to check multiple organizations first. We did not know anyone who had walked this particular path, and we were incredibly ignorant about so many things. For example, we did not even know that there would be no financial cost to us, and instead we would get paid a per diem for foster care and then an adoption subsidy even after we finalized.

Annie: We started with the idea that we would consider taking a placement only if the child was already in the permanent custody of the State and clearly available to be adopted, but that first night of training changed everything. I feel like it was the first

Appendix 10

time in my life that my heart was broken for the things that break the Lord's heart. It was no longer about us and our heartache and sorrow. It was about kids out there who need love. We had no idea what might happen, but we quickly determined that we would be open to whatever role God had for us. We would be a revolving door if necessary because there are kids out there who are not safe. It didn't matter to us whether we would have them for a couple days or for a long time.

Both: Our friends were supportive and prayed with us, but our parents were scared. In retrospect we gave them too much information about why foster care has such a need and about the percentages of kids who are abused. So they worried about what could happen to David and whether we were endangering him! We were not trying to be naïve, but we also realized that there were kids who desperately needed help, so how could we let fear make us say that it was someone else's responsibility? We trusted God to protect our family, yet we also had wisdom in the parameters that we set by keeping David as the oldest and biggest.

Jon: We dove into the licensing process, completing all of our training and paperwork during the summer. By August we were certified and receiving calls about possible placements, none of which materialized. We took in some children for short respites in September, and the calls kept coming.

Annie: Unlike the relatively predictable process and timeline when I was pregnant with David, with this we never knew what might come next. Every call made me so emotional. In the moment I wanted to say yes to everything, but that is impossible. One call was for a sibling group of four kids, and we did not even have a vehicle large enough to seat everybody. Ultimately, we made a list outlining what we realistically could and could not accept. Since Jon was the practical and steady one, he would return the calls to the social worker.

Jon: Late in September we were contacted about an atypical placement. With six older siblings already in State custody, both Marissa and Nate had been born straight in to foster care. At ages three and two, they were available to be adopted. Previously, their foster mom had adopted one of their older brothers, and she wanted to adopt them, but the agency had concerns that she was ill-equipped to parent three children. Already Marissa and Nate were showing significant medical, social, and emotional issues due to her incompetence. Nate could barely walk and was unable to eat solid food. Marissa had major social anxiety and significant speech delays. So they asked us to take the children for respite weekends over the next several months, with the plan that if all went well, we would adopt them. It was complicated because the foster mom was not told what was happening, and when she figured it out, she filed false reports about us to try to stop the placement.

Both: Nonetheless by December the children were placed with us full time. We had to do immediate triage with their medical care because they were continually sick and plagued with all kinds of infections. In the nine months until the adoption finalized, we had a constant stream of workers coming to the house along with weekly paperwork. In that window of time we were not in control of our lives but were at the whim of anyone who needed to have a meeting.

Jon: It was so difficult during those months not to have the full authority to make decisions for the children we knew were going to be ours.

Annie: Once we finalized there were different challenges. I struggled to bond with them. It was especially tough coming through the fostering process because there were so many moving pieces. But in moments when I do not feel love for them, I have learned to ask God to give me love and to help me to see them the way he does. It is also hard to clean up a mess we did not create, and I have struggled with my anger toward the foster mom and with other people's judgments of Marissa's and Nate's behavior. Sometimes my pride makes me want to announce, "They're adopted, and we haven't had them since the beginning," so that people do not think their delays are a reflection of me.

Both: We have never regretted it, but we have certainly felt overwhelmed and questioned how to parent them. In those times God has reminded us that he will continue to equip us. He has graciously given us Scripture and support, and just reminded us to obey.

Jon: It is a humbling experience to work with their special needs. It is sanctifying, and when you are at a point of frustration, the only place to turn is God.

Both: Even though Marissa and Nate know that they are adopted, because of their cognitive delays we are not sure what they understand. We do celebrate Gotcha Day and Adoption Day with special dinners, cake, and friends and family. As worried as they were, once our families met Marissa and Nate and knew the placement would be permanent, they were completely on board.

Annie: David has a Christmas ornament celebrating "Baby's First Christmas." Once we adopted Marissa and Nate, I searched for something similar for them. It grieved me to come up empty-handed. But God knew my heart. An acquaintance spotted the last "Adoption 2014" ornament on a store shelf, and she felt the Lord compel her to buy it for us. I just cried, and I cherish it so much.

Overall we are grateful that Marissa and Nate are young enough that they really have blended right in our home and do not have much memory of their earlier years. We do not plan to keep their story from them, but we will reveal additional details as they are able to understand. Occasionally they talk about their previous foster mom, but not often. They have pictures of their brother who still lives there, and they are supposed to see him monthly, but his mom cancels that a lot. Overall they just gel in our world, and the outside observer would never know that they came by adoption.

Jon: The best part of this experience has been seeing how God has redeemed our pain through them, and knowing that God will redeem their difficult beginnings through our family.

Annie: I have learned so much more about redemption through this process. I grew up in the church, but things that were just words before have been acted out now. I am adopted into God's family. That word gets to my heart differently now. And the idea of being chosen is more meaningful. When we had David, we did not have to fight for him. But in adopting Marissa and Nate, there is a different kind of love. We have fought for them out of choice, not obligation.

Annie: Already one couple we know has become certified as foster parents because of our story. I am very vocal about how I think Christians need to get involved in foster care. So much destruction happens in the early years for some of these kids that I believe we need Christians to come in and help restore what's been lost. And our experience has opened people's eyes to the fact that some foster care does have the adoptive end.

Jon: We also know how different our story is from many other people that come through the foster-to-adopt process, but we feel that God has really blessed our family over and above what we could have dreamed. We trust that God will use our testimony for his purposes.

www.ingramcontent.com/pod-product-compliance
Lightning Source LLC
Chambersburg PA
CBHW031502160426
43195CB00010BB/1078